**Exploring Maya 4
30 Studies in 3D**

Maximilian Schönherr

Exploring Maya 4

30 Studies in 3D

Peachpit Press

Exploring Maya 4: 30 Studies in 3D
Maximilian Schönherr

Peachpit Press
1249 Eighth Street
Berkeley, CA 94710
510.524.2178
510.524.2221 (fax)

Find us on the World Wide Web at www.peachpit .com
To report errors, please send a note to errata@peachpit.com
Peachpit Press is a division of Pearson Education

First published in the German language under the title *Maya 4 Sketches* by Addison-Wesley,
an imprint of Pearson Education Deutschland GmbH, München.

U.S. Editor: Nancy Davis
Copyeditor: Kate McKinley
Production Coordinator: Myrna Vladic
Compositor: Jude Levinson
Indexer: Emily Glossbrenner

ISBN: 0-201-74216-0
0 9 8 7 6 5 4 3 2 1
Printed and bound in the United States of America

TABLE OF CONTENTS

FOREWORD

"It is just the little touches
after the average man would quit
that make the master's fame "

—Orison Swett Marden

How true it is and yet, how hard for that average man to see. No matter how great the master, all were beginners at one point (though many of them love to forget that fact). It doesn't take much rummaging around in a master's past *oeuvre* to find enough crude works to prove my point.

Sometimes the difference between a master craftsman and a layman is minimal. Take bricklayers. The master takes the extra few minutes to carefully lay a plumbline, or has three extra sizes of grouting knives and a double-handled scraper with supertips. This analogy holds exactly true, especially now in new-media and cutting-edge production: Invest in your tools! Computer modeling already requires such immense expenditures of effort, time, energy, nerves, and cash that it's really "pound-foolish" not to invest the extra 0.2 percent to truly learn those nuances that make the difference between a Maya layman and a Maya master.

Creative growth comes in fits and starts. At every plateau an artist needs some small push to reach the next new ideas. But where do the masters get these inspirations? What is the source of true "newness"? Real inspiration can't be forced and it can't be bought, but now and then it can be found in the words and pictures of a book. Like this one. For the price of an average meal, the budding Maya master can strap on little rocket shoes for a push into the creative stratosphere!

I know Max Schönherr going back to his days as a journalist and tinkerer, long before his first tome. That his name has become synonymous with deciphering Maya is lovely to see. You can bet it didn't happen without a lot of "sweat equity" on his part. You can find no better guide to Maya than he.

Of course, even with this fine book, there is no substitute for experience. You simply have to jump right in: Kill the nights and drift along; immerse your-self entirely until all the little tips and tricks truly condense into knowledge, indexed and instantly recallable. You can't just flip through a book like this and leave it on the shelf; you have to roll up your sleeves and get deeply into it.

Then why not take the next step? Ping the author (email is such a lovely thing, much more polite than disturbing him over breakfast). When you come up with new questions—or answers—don't be shy. Max has invested months of his life in this heap of molecules, putting his thoughts and images into book form so he can share his knowledge; he'll be delighted if something comes back as well. And send me your results, too; I'm always interested!

SO DO IT ALREADY! Don't just stand there, buy this book. What you learn here just might mean that the next project (you know the one— yeah, that one, the big one) may be killer and not just so-so.

In that spirit, have fun being creative!

Kai Krause
www.byteburg.net

Photo: Birgit Klemt, Hamburg
Byteburg Rheineck

INTRODUCTION

A year ago I wrote a German book about the aesthetics of 3D animation using Maya—a much more basic book than this one. That book contained 12 brief tutorials which I called "sketches" (and in German, that term has mainly its comic meaning of a short, funny dialog). They were randomly sprinkled in among the 600 pages of more fundamental and comprehensive information; mini-chapters not at all related to the rest and extremely satisfying to write. After having completed a massive chapter about the basics of character animation or logic nodes, I looked forward to inserting a sketch where I could play: set a cube on fire, make the crescent moon rise, or create a will-o'-the-wisp. Islands of pleasure.

This new book contains no basics whatsoever, just islands of pleasure. If you're familiar with the Maya interface you'll enjoy the tutorials as much as I have. Each chapter is based on an everyday question, as it might cross our minds: How do I roll a ball over a mountain? How do I get the shadow of a birch tree (with all the trembling leaves and branches) inside my spartan little 3D room? How does a volcano erupt? How do I make a character steer a bicycle while waving hello to me? How do I animate Chinese calligraphy for an educational CD-ROM? How do I simulate a crash test for cars?

None of the 30 tutorials of this book will take up more than an hour of your time—that's all you need to make the crater spew fire or see the cyclist wave. But my experience with students suggests that each chapter will invoke parallel ideas, create spin-offs so that at the end of the day, quite different and much more elaborate things evolve. And since the tutorials aren't linked to specific software tools or techniques, but rather to questions derived from real life, you'll find you return to the book again and again. When working on a totally different project, you'll suddenly remember that doorbell button or the knobbly guy.

Completed computer animations for film, television, computer games, or the Web are usually complex, and the Maya scenes behind them are rich with geometry, textures, and lights. In this book each chapter starts at zero. When in Chapter 21 you throw a (Maya Cloth) poncho over a torso, you don't need to model an elaborate human body or load a heavy scene file from CD in order to start. A sphere with a slightly scaled down north pole to indicate the nape of the neck is enough to go into the poncho's single hole and make the fabric rest comfortably on the skin. In Chapter 8 you won't find a wonderfully textured cyclist—you'll just use a few clicks to model the top part of a human skeleton, with arms and shoulders. You don't need more than that to learn about constraints and study steering with one or two hands. Certainly, you can load the results of all 30 chapters from the CD. The CD also contains rendered movies you might want to study to see things in action, in motion— something books these days can't show you.

The majority of the tutorials can be completed with the basic version of Maya. Where more advanced tools from the Unlimited version are required, you'll find hints for getting the same or similar results with the tools you have at hand. The book refers to version 4 of Maya, which came out in summer 2001, and makes heavy use of new technologies like Nonlinear Animation with Clips, Poses, the Trax Editor, Subdivision Surfaces for modeling, and digital painting with the Paint Effects—not because these technologies are hip, but because they make workflows much more economic and, even better, more satisfying. Modeling the leg of a crooked chair or a pair of nostrils with Subdivision Surfaces is, compared to previous techniques, nothing less than an interactive delight.

Despite its playfulness, the book doesn't balk at mathematics because the regular use of random expressions, If conditions, and sine functions can dramatically ease the daily animation routine. Many chapters include these expressions. MEL, on the other hand, has no place here. MEL is a programming language with a massive syntax and command set, and it requires too much specialized knowledge far beyond the scope of this rather popular and "light" book. Game developers, who in the last couple of months seem to have embraced Maya, won't learn here how to build and animate Lara Croft X, but the broad concept of the book will provide inspiration about all the fundamental parts of Maya for their daily work.

The book, like the software itself, is structured in the four classic parts: Animation, Modeling, Dynamics, and Rendering. You'll find the Paint Effects under Rendering, Cloth under Dynamics, the crooked chair under Modeling, and the ball rolling (and not sliding!) over a mountain under Animation. Nonlinear Animation, however, is such a widely applicable technology that it's spread throughout the book. So use the index! The sequence in which the chapters appear has nothing to do with difficulty levels or degrees of sophistication, only with change and variation. Just dive into the chapters that jump out at you as you browse.

Obviously, 200 some odd pages of paper can't compete with the terabytes of information on the Internet. On the other hand, you can't casually pick up the Internet and put it on your lap in the garden. Most information related to Maya on the Web isn't very well organized, though it's rich in mass and content. You'll find dozens of tutorials and hundreds of free MEL scripts and plug-ins under the hood of www.highend3d.com and www.aliaswavefront.com, just to name the two most important sites. Also, this book is being accompanied and extended in the Internet. Visit the Web sites of the publisher (www.peachpit.com) and the author (www.aquinofilm.de/maya) to find out more.

Cologne, Germany, Fall 2001

Maximilian Schönherr
max.schoenherr@uni-koeln.de

ANIMATION

PLEASE TURN THE PAGE

How do I turn the page of a book in 3D?
Theme: Animation
Techniques and tools used: EP Curve, Loft

This first tutorial is by far the most lightweight in this book. You may even find the task of turning the page of a book in 3D trivial and even boring. That's what I thought as well—until I presented this task to ten university students in a 3D-animation class. I gave them 30 minutes to model a sheet of paper and turn it over from right to left.

Some of the students already animated 3D characters in their spare time, others paid their rent with jobs in Web design. All of them were up to speed

in the Maya interface—but in half an hour, no one managed to construct a curved book page that could be turned. The best result was a convex page that penetrated parts of the book because its curvature didn't change as it was turned. Some of the students tried to attack the problem with Soft Body Dynamics, one student even wanted to use Maya Cloth; they just couldn't handle the problem using basic modeling techniques.

So if you still find this tutorial trivial, go ahead and construct a page on your computer now. And don't turn the page of this book until you succeed in turning your 3D page in Maya.

You don't need Soft Body Dynamics to turn a page in 3D. And you don't have to deal with tediously selecting and moving CVs, either. Like so many other problems, there are several possible solutions, but only a few are elegantly simple. To find this solution, take a step back. Don't think about modeling the page, just concentrate on the heart of the matter—which is animation, not modeling.

This animation consists of a rotation around the center axis of the book, where the pages meet. If you start by modeling this page with, for example, a primitive Nurbs Plane and try to rotate it around that axis, you'll have to deal with CVs in order to get the proper curvature. Nothing against doing it this way! Keep in mind, though, that CVs should be used only at the finest level of modeling and mainly for subtle changes, but kept out of basic procedures. So the best way doesn't start with the plane in this case, it starts with curves. Since we're dealing with rotation around an axis, all we really need are three curves parallel to that axis.

1　In the Top View, create three parallel curves using the EP Curve Tool (Figure 1.1). The third curve should lie along the Z-axis. This is the line where the book pages join, and is therefore our axis of rotation.
2　Create a Loft over all three curves (Figure 1.2).
3　Hide the third curve (the book's spine).
4　Create an animation length of 200 frames.

Notice that all of the curves pivot at the center of the scene, which also is the center of our book. You can check this by selecting the curves, then looking at the rotation or translation tools. If the pivot is somewhere else, use the Insert mode to change it to the middle.

5　Test your page by rotating the first two curves together (not the lofted surface) around the Z-axis.
6　Go to the start of the timeline and set a keyframe for the Z-rotation of the first two curves (right-click Rotate Z in the Channel Box, then click Key Selected) (Figure 1.3).
7　Go to the end of the animation. Rotate both curves by −180° in Z and set another keyframe.

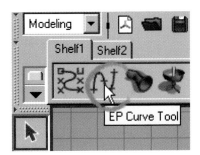

▲　*Figure 1.1 Using the EP Curve Tool you can create Nurbs curves with only two clicks.*

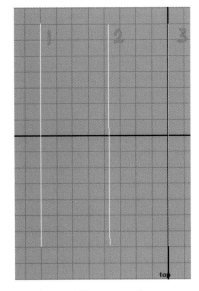

▲　*Figure 1.2 Three curves for one book page.*

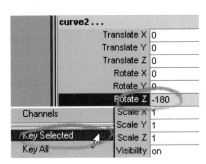

▲　*Figure 1.3 Two keyframes for the curves make the page turn.*

Figure 1.4 Although it looks like the ▶ page itself is being rotated, it's really only the curves that move.

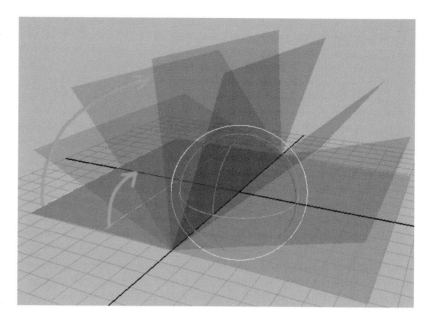

When you play back the animation it feels a little stiff, but in principal it works: It shows a page turning (Figure 1.4). Now we'll give the surface the characteristic curvature of a book page. There's a hidden trap here. Normally, we think in terms of translations ("I lift the glass to my mouth," instead of " I rotate the glass around the axis of my elbow"). So the temptation is to move the middle curve upward, instead of rotating it (Figure 1.5).

Figure 1.5 When dealing with a rotation, translating the middle curve upwards is taboo. ▼

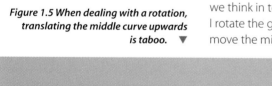

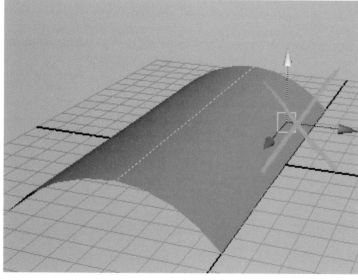

1 Go to the start of the animation.
2 Select the middle curve, and rotate it around Z until you like the curvature of the surface.
3 Set a keyframe for Rotate Z.
4 Go to the end of the animation.
5 Rotate the curve back to get a nice bend in the other direction.
6 Set a key for Rotate Z.

You can best see the turning and bending of the page in the Side View window (Figure 1.6).

By simply rotating a few things and translating nothing, we now have the turning of the page under control. From here on you can add more detail to the animation: first at the level of the curve rotation and timing (the outer curve starts turning earlier and stops turning later than the middle curve) and only then at the level of CVs (maybe add a dog-eared page or give the impression of an invisible hand plucking the page at one corner).

You cannot rotate CVs, you can only translate them. So you might want to consider assembling selected CVs in Clusters (you'll find the Create Cluster command in the animation section F2 under Deform). Clusters of CVs have rotation pivots that you can move anywhere you like.

Now you have a page, but where is the book? Begin by duplicating the

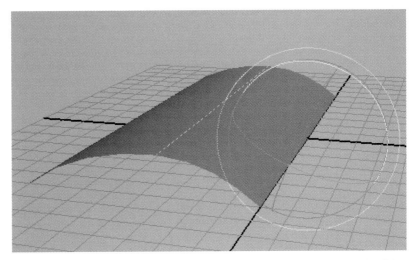

▲ *Figure 1.6 The correct way to bend the paper is to rotate the middle curve.*

curves you already have, in their start and end positions. Create a couple of lofted, planar surfaces and the book is finished within minutes (Figure 1.7). If the audience will see the page from both sides, you'll have to put some extra work into texturing it. The normal way of texturing makes the page look the same on both sides. There is a straightforward way to apply double-sided shading to the Nurbs surface, which you'll find in the online documentation by searching for "double-sided shading."

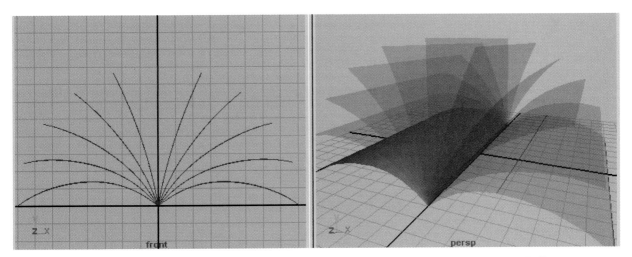

▲ *Figure 1.7 Two curves, each with two keyframes...and the page turns over nicely.*

And now for something completely different: Ever dragged a light from the Outliner into the Perspective Window using the middle mouse button?

How do I stir up super clean camera movement?
Theme: Animation
Techniques and tools used: Create Clip, Trax Editor

Nonlinear animation is nothing more than shifting, stretching, and crossfading animation data just as we do with video editing software. The technique has only recently been implemented in Maya as the Trax Editor, a great new animation tool that in many cases replaces the Graph Editor and the Dope Sheet.

The Dope Sheet is still the ideal place to move keyframes around in time. The Graph Editor is indispensable for controlling the before and after of keyframes. But whenever previously set keyframes have to be moved or mixed together, nonlinear animation with the Trax Editor is the way to go.

Imagine you've animated a camera smoothly, spent a lot of time fine-tuning the keyframes' tangents to make the camera move faster. Then your client comes in and says he's just seen one of those beautifully experimental "Dogma" films from Denmark and would you please make your 3D camera's movement a little rougher. Instead of the typical immaculately smooth 3D movement, he'd rather see a shaky camera—like a steadycam maybe—that basically follows the same track as your existing camera does, of course, but looks, well, a little more improvised.

In the old days you would have opened the Graph Editor and inserted additional keyframes to shake up the camera motion. To get this right, you would have had to invest a lot of effort, and besides that, your work would have been destructive: By inserting new keyframes into your existing animation you throw away the smooth motion of the camera. If, when you had

Figure 2.1 This is smooth camera ▶
motion toward a cone. I used the
command Create Motion Trail to get the
graphic representation of the motion
path with numbered keyframes.

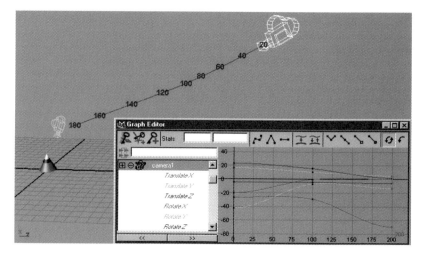

finished all this, the client complained that this was *too* much Dogma style, you would have to re-do the whole thing from scratch.

With the arrival of nonlinear animation, you have the ability to present several versions of more or less shaky camera motions to your client almost immediately, without destroying a single keyframe of your existing animation.

1 Prepare an animation length of 200 frames.

2 Create a camera and an object the camera can move toward.

3 Animate the motion of the camera toward the object with two or more keyframes (for its beginning, middle, and end). Feel free to create a slightly curved motion path.

4 Delete all animation channels where nothing happens, by choosing Edit > Delete by Type > Static Channels.

5 Edit the remaining keys in the Graph Editor. For example, you may want to flatten the tangents of the start and end keyframes and convert the tangents of the middle keyframes to "spline."

6 Open the Create Clip Options window by pressing F2 and choosing Animate > Create Clip ⬛. This is the window where you shift from classic keyframing to nonlinear animation. Enter a name for the smooth-camera animation here.

7 Click the Create Clip button. You now have a clip, and since you left the settings in the window unchanged, the keyframes disappear from the Time-line. Nevertheless, the camera moves, because the animation data are handled by the Trax Editor.

8 Open the Trax Editor: Choose Window > Animation Editors > Trax Editor (Figure 2.2).

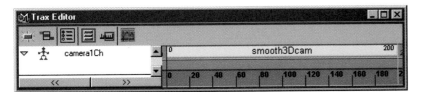

◄ *Figure 2.2 The animation channels of the smooth camera are now a clip in the Trax Editor.*

The camera motion data are now assembled as a horizontal bar in the one and only track of the Trax Editor. That track—you can see it on the left side of the Trax Editor—belongs to a new character that Maya has created. You don't have to worry about it now, although the character plays an important role in animation generally, because it can incorporate many parameters of several objects. This especially makes the animation of complex 3D creatures or systems much more efficient. In our case, however, the character consists of nothing but a couple of camera translation and rotation channels.

Use the context menu of the right mouse button to deactivate the camera motion in the Trax Editor by unchecking Enable Clip. Now the camera will stay where you left it, so you can do other things with it. You won't lose its animation data. We'll create a brief animation sequence where the camera just shakes.

1 Switch to the perspective view.

2 Go to the beginning of the animation. The camera doesn't move, it stays where you left it when you disabled the clip.

3 In the Channel Box, set the three Translate and three Rotate Channels of the camera to 0. The camera jumps to the origin of the scene.

4 Set a keyframe for the camera (or even better, just for its translation and rotation).

5 Set a keyframe at frame 20 for the same parameters.

6 Go to frame 5, move and rotate the camera slightly. Set a key.

7 Create more keys for slightly changed translation and rotation channels at frames 10 and 15.

When you play back the animation, the camera still sits at the origin and doesn't go anywhere. But it doesn't sit still, it shakes and turns quite dramatically for less than a second. Now we'll convert these channels into a new clip.

1 Choose Animation > Create Clip, and in the Create Clip Options window create a clip for the new animation and give it a shaky name (Figure 2.3).

Once again the keyframe marks disappear from the timeline. You can still access the animation data in the Trax Editor. The shaky clip shows up there right underneath the clip for the smooth camera motion. Since we made it only 20 frames long, the bar representing the shaky camera is much shorter than the bar for the original 200-frame camera motion.

2 Right-click on the smooth-camera clip and choose Enable Clip to re-enable the original clip (Figure 2.4).

3 Look through the camera.

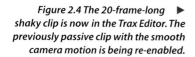

Figure 2.3 Make the clip for your ▲
shaky camera using the Create Clip
Options window.

Figure 2.4 The 20-frame-long ▶
shaky clip is now in the Trax Editor. The
previously passive clip with the smooth
camera motion is being re-enabled.

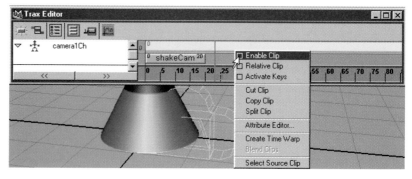

When you play back the animation, you see the original camera motion, but with a very shaky start. Give your camera a few frames of peace before it starts shaking, by moving the shaky clip a little to the right.

Now the camera starts shaking later on its journey toward the cone. Most likely, the shaking effect is much too strong. Let's smooth it out a little:

● Double-click the shaky clip to bring up its parameters in the Channel Box. Try reducing its Weight from 1 to a value of 0.2 (Figure 2.5).

If you left-click to enlarge the clip to the length of the whole animation, it won't stretch. It will loop. A Dogma camera like the one your client has in mind does not shake all the time, it has smooth moments as well on its path to the object of desire.

In the Trax Editor, copy the shaky clip using the right mouse button and the Copy Clip command. Choose Edit > Paste to insert it. You'll find the duplicated clip in a new, third track. Move it up to the second track in the middle of the animation.

If you double-click the clip and its weight still shows *1* in the Channel Box, reduce it to your taste.

You can make the shaky clips longer by changing their Scale in the Channel Box. Try 3 for one clip. A Scale of 3 spreads the clips to three times their original length without looping them, so the camera shakes don't come immediately after each other.

Duplicate the shaky clip again and move the new one to the end of the animation so the camera still keeps shaking after reaching its final position.

When you play back the animation, you realize that after frame 200, when the smooth camera sends out no more information about its position, the last shaky clip takes over and makes the camera jump to the origin. That's where it was created. The jump has to do with absolute and relative position values. In Relative mode the animation parameters of the shaky camera are not treated as they are but added to the data of the other clip. Right-click the shaky clip at the end of the animation and check Relative Clip (Figure 2.6).

shakeCam	
Weight	0.2
Enable	on
Offset	absolute
Start Frame	32
Cycle	1
Scale	1
Start	0
Duration	20

▲ *Figure 2.5 The shaking effect becomes less drastic when its weight is reduced.*

◀ *Figure 2.6 After frame 200, the camera gets information only from the shaky clips which were generated at the origin—so the camera jumps right there. Fix this by setting the last shaky clip to Relative Clip. Now the camera reaches its final position and still shakes a little.*

You can apply the Relative Clip command to other clips as well. If you hadn't created the shaking movement at the origin but somewhere else in space, you would *have* to set all clips in that track to relative.

With the help of nonlinear animation you've created a very flexible Dogma camera without losing your original smooth animation. If your customer changes his mind again and wants an extremely shaky camera in the middle of the path, you now know where to click—and you only need to change a single parameter. The Trax Editor is as flexible as the editing window of video editing software. As in video editing you can also crossfade clips (see Chapter 6 for more on this).

And now for something completely different: Ever made bones thin?

FUN WITH A TWIST

How do I deform a cube out of all recognition?
Theme: Animation, Modeling
Techniques and tools used: Nonlinear Deformers—
Bend, Flare, Sine, Squash, Twist, Wave

An example of a *linear* deformation is scaling an object along the X-axis. We use this technique all the time in computer animation when we make houses narrower or taller or make spheres bigger. With *nonlinear* deformation we don't manipulate the object uniformly along a single axis. Nonlinear deformations can be used in both animation and modeling. Using the Bend Deformer for example, you can very easily animate an object bending around a corner. You don't even have to touch a single CV. If you would like to widen the middle of a previously modeled object, just use the Squash Deformer.

You'll find these valuable tools under the F2 animation menu in the "nonlinear" section. Actually, several other deformers, such as the Sculpt Deformer, behave in a nonlinear way, but are not grouped into this section. We're going to try out some of them by using the six main nonlinear deformers to heavily distort a simple polygon cube.

Before we start, let's detach the entire menu of nonlinear deformers so we have them handy at all times. You need the main menubar to detach individual menus or submenus, so if you don't see the main Maya menubar at the top of your screen, choose Hotbox Controls > Window Options > Show Main Menubar. Now switch to the F2 animation menu set, and detach the Create Nonlinear pull-down menu from the Deform menu by clicking on its separator lines, as shown in Figure 3.1. Move the little window to the side of your perspective viewport. It will float on top of that window. You can hide the main menubar now, if you wish.

You now have six deformer tools at hand. First we'll create a cube and bend it around a corner using the Bend Deformer.

1 Create a polygon cube, enlarge it to 10 units in all three directions, and give it 10 Subdivisions in each direction.
2 Animate the cube so that it starts at frame 0 with X = −35 on the left, and ends after 200 frames at X = 35 on the right.
3 Go to frame 20. Select the cube and in the floating menu, click Bend (Figure 3.2).

Like most deformation tools, Bend shows no change at first—but that's no reason to turn our back on it. Take a look at the deformation tool in wireframe mode. It's sitting inside the cube.

1 Under the Input section of the Channel Box, open *bend1* and change its Curvature from 0 to 1.

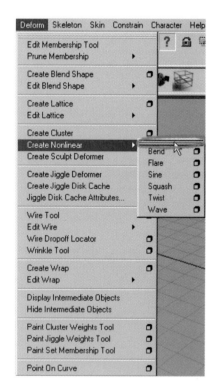

Figure 3.1 Detaching the submenu of ▲
nonlinear deformers.

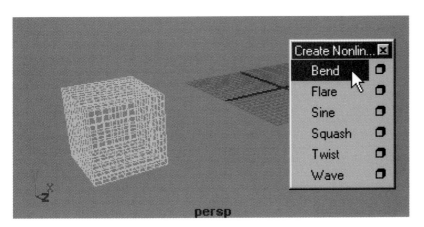

◄ *Figure 3.2 The cube is under the influence of the Bend Deformer. The floating window to the right is the menu of nonlinear deformers.*

2 Press the T key, so the three manipulators for *bend1* appear, as in Figure 3.3. Play with them.

3 Rotate *bend1* by 90 degrees around Z.

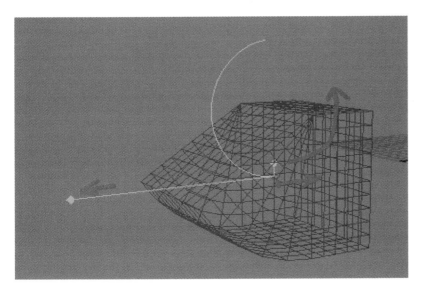

◄ *Figure 3.3 The three manipulators of the Bend Deformer make the cube bend around the corner.*

When you play back the animation, the cube is being bent around the curve tangentially to its motion path. After your cube turns the corner, move the *bend1* manipulator so that the cube moves along the X axis, leaving the deformer's area of influence. Or you can just go to the Channel Box and reduce the value for Low Bound to *0*. Let's try another deformer.

1 Go to a frame where your cube has left the influence of *bend1*, and apply the Flare Deformer.

2 Rotate *flare1* by 90 degrees around Z.

3 Click on *flare1* in the Channel Box, press the *T* key, and move its seven manipulators (Figure 3.4).

Figure 3.4 The Flare Deformer ▶
narrows the cube's center.

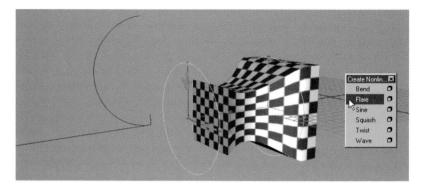

As you can see, Flare can make the cube thinner or thicker at its entrance and exit (Start and End Flare) and it can add a dent or bulge (Curve) all around the middle. The Low and High Bound are responsible for how widely the effect spreads.

Scrub through the animation to see how the cube shoves itself first through *bend1* and then through *flare1*. In the Channel Box, set the values of both Start and End Flare to *1* so that the cube keeps its original size as it enters and leaves the deformer. Give Curve a slightly negative value like –0.5 to narrow the cube in the middle of the Flare Deformer.

1 After the cube leaves *flare1*, just before the middle of the animation range, apply the Sine Deformer to it (Figure 3.5).

Figure 3.5 Sine makes the cube wavy ▶
in one dimension.

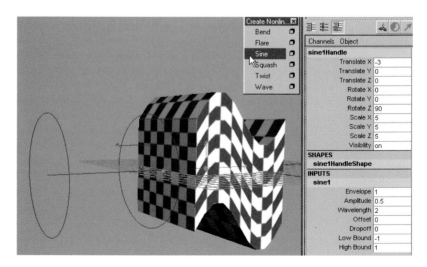

2 Like you did with the others, rotate *sine1* by 90 degrees around Z and raise its Amplitude from 0 to 0.5.

3 Play with the manipulators of *sine1*.

The wavelength not only determines how frequently the waves appear but also how our cube enters and leaves the deformation. A wavelength of 0.5 or 3.1 is not equal to a multiple of a complete oscillation and therefore changes the shape of the cube before and after the deformation. Set the Wavelength of *sine1* to an integer (a whole number) like 1 or 2.

1 After the cube leaves *sine1*'s influence, apply the Squash Deformer.

2 Rotate it by 90 degrees around Z so the direction of its influence tilts in the same direction the cube is going during its way through its animation path.

The most important parameter for the Squash effect is its strength, or Factor. Unlike Flare, which narrows or widens certain regions of an object without affecting the rest of it, Squash tries to maintain the same volume. In other words, when Squash compresses the middle of an object, it will widen the outer regions, and vice versa. The classic application for this is a bouncing ball which, when it touches the ground, is squeezed vertically and at the same time becomes wider.

Negative squash factors imply a thickening effect, which makes the whole cube shorter (see Figure 3.6). If you chose a squash factor of *1*, the cube is being compressed but stretched at the same time. Start and End Smoothness give you the option to ease the effect in and out more or less smoothly. With a value of *0* the effect grabs the cube suddenly, whereas a value of *1* lets the effect start gently. When you're happy with your Squash settings, move a little on in the Timeline and we'll try the next deformer.

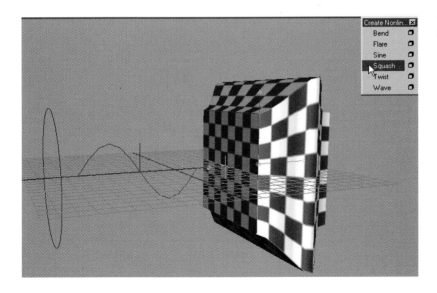

◄ *Figure 3.6 Squash thickens and shortens the cube at the same time.*

1 Apply the Twist Deformer to the cube.

2 Rotate it by 90 degrees around Z.

Twist is the first deformer in our assemblage that rotates the cube itself. The crucial manipulators for this rotation are the yellow circles that let you set the amount of rotation at the beginning and the end (see Figure 3.7). Note that Start and End Angle influence the cube's rotation before it enters and after it leaves the Twist Deformer. If the cube comes in with an angle other than 0 (in our composition this is the End Angle), all previous deformations are performed, rotated by this angle. Low and High Bound, as before, determine the limits of the effect. A high value for Envelope doesn't make the effect stronger but widens its range of influence. This is the same for all deformers.

Figure 3.7 With the Twist Deformer's manipulators you can adjust the inner rotation of the cube. ▶

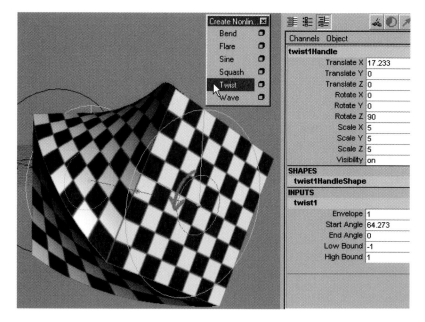

● Toward the end of the animation, apply the Wave Deformer to the cube.

The Wave Deformer doesn't have to be rotated. You can see its effect at once by raising the Amplitude of *wave1* from 0 to 1 (see Figure 3.8). This is a very sensitive parameter, so a value of 0.2 can be much more attractive than higher values. The use of manipulators comes in very handy here as well. Note the difference between the Sine and Wave Deformers: Sine makes the object wavy in one dimension, but Wave makes it oscillate in two dimensions.

If you chose a higher resolution for the cube, you can use the deformers for high-level animation and modeling. For example, Twist can be used to create a screw. With Wave, you can animate water surfaces like oceans. Note that you can have as many deformers as you like working together at the same place on the same object. Try mixing several Wave deformers together

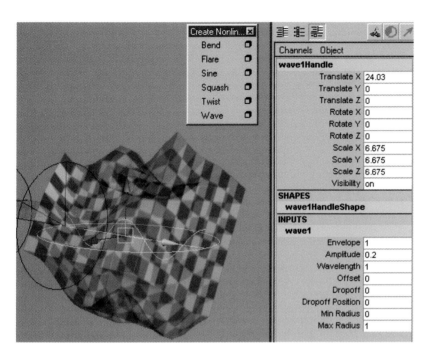

Create Nonlin... ☒		
Bend	▢	
Flare	▢	
Sine	▢	
Squash	▢	
Twist	▢	
Wave	▢	

Channels Object	
wave1Handle	
Translate X	24.03
Translate Y	0
Translate Z	0
Rotate X	0
Rotate Y	0
Rotate Z	0
Scale X	6.675
Scale Y	6.675
Scale Z	6.675
Visibility	on
SHAPES	
wave1HandleShape	
INPUTS	
wave1	
Envelope	1
Amplitude	0.2
Wavelength	1
Offset	0
Dropoff	0
Dropoff Position	0
Min Radius	0
Max Radius	1

◀ *Figure 3.8 The two-dimensional wave and its deformation victim shown in X-ray shading mode.*

Figure 3.9 Six cool deformations for a
▼ *simple cube.*

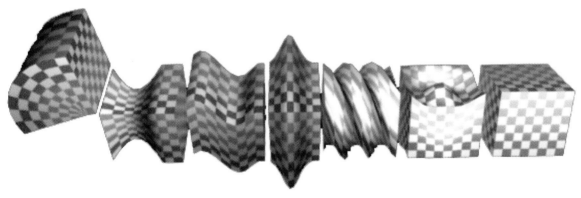

to create ripples within ripples of large waves. Or move the Wave Deformer to where Twist does its work and you can have a strong twist combined with a subtle wavy effect (Figure 3.9).

In addition, instead of moving the cube you can animate the deformers—not only their position but also all other parameters, for example to fade the deformation effects in and out. Run the animation and stop at the effects you like best, then duplicate the cube there and create Blend Shapes out of these deformations. With this tool you can interactively blend different states of the object with each other by using (and of course keying) Blend Shape sliders. Imagine this procedure with character animation!

And now for something completely different: Know what happens when you right-click in the Timeline?

RRRRING THE BELL

How can I make a bell ring by pressing a knob?
Theme: Animation
Techniques and tools used: Nurbs Modeling, Random and If-Then Expressions, Set Driven Key, Channel Control

Maya can't actually produce ringing sounds, of course, but we can use it to make a clapper that will vibrate against a bell. And we can build a ringer knob that, when pressed, makes the clapper vibrate. This tutorial is about animation and dependencies. But it's also about working as one animator in a team and preparing a scene in such a way that a colleague who specializes in character animation will understand it right away. Here we deal with reduction, with hiding from view anything that might distract the person dealing with the 3D-character who will press the knob to ring the bell for entry to the house.

First, model four objects: the bell itself, a clapper for the bell, a knob, and a frame for the knob.

You can just use Primitives since this tutorial is not about complex modeling. The geometry in Figure 4.1 was created this way. The ringer body is the upper half of a Nurbs sphere, scaled slightly flatter. The clapper consists of a Nurbs cylinder, a lengthy surface created with the Square Tool and lofts for its thickness. These parts were grouped together so that they don't lose contact when being rotated. The frame of the ringer knob was created by applying the Round Tool to a Nurbs cube. The knob itself is the rescaled half of a Nurbs sphere, similar to the bell. Let's work on the motion of the clapper first.

Figure 4.1 A simple setup for a ringer ▶
device with a bell, a clapper, a knob,
and a frame.

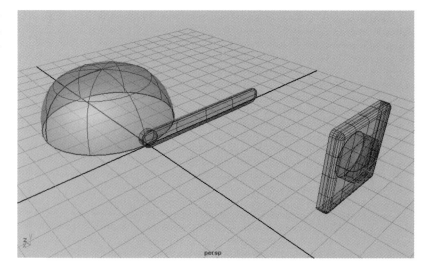

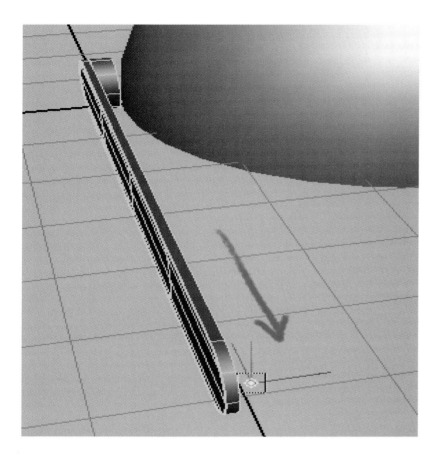

1 Select the clapper (actually the group that contains all of the clapper's surfaces) and in Insert mode move its pivot to the back (see Figure 4.2).
2 In the Channel Box, click *Rotate Y* for the clapper, and use the context menu of the right mouse button to open the Expression Editor (see Figure 4.3).
3 Type the following expression in the empty lower field and substitute *ringerG* with the name you chose for your clapper assembly:

```
ringerG.rotateY = rand (-0.5, 0.5);
```

4 Activate the expression by clicking Create.

The clapper now rotates randomly between plus half a degree and minus half a degree around its vertical axis. If the rattling is too weak for your setup, increase the values in the brackets of the random function *rand*.

If we could hear it, the bell would ring constantly now, without a break. But what we want it to do is ring only when the red knob is being pressed. In order to achieve this we will have to create a dependency between the position of the knob and the on/off state of the random expression. First we need a new attribute for on and off.

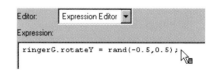

▲ *Figure 4.3 A random expression makes the clapper rotate between −0.5 and 0.5 degrees.*

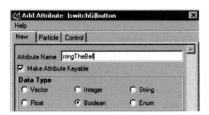

*Figure 4.4 The knob receives a new ▲
attribute for pressed/not pressed.*

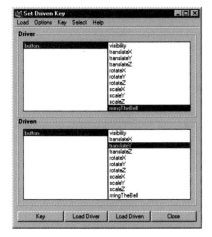

*Figure 4.5 Set Driven Key creates a ▲
relationship between the position of the
knob (its translateY value here) and the
on/off value of the new ringer attribute
(rrringTheBell). Unlike normal keyframes,
Set Driven Keys are not correlations
between attributes and time, but between
attributes and attributes.*

1 Open the knob's Attribute Editor and choose Attributes > Add Attribute to open the window for creating a new attribute for the object (Figure 4.4).
2 Give the attribute a name, such as *rrringTheBell*, set its Data Type to Boolean (which means 0 or 1, off or on, with no choices in between; a Data Type of Integer would accept all whole numbers and give us too many choices) and click OK to create the attribute.

You'll find the new attribute right underneath the attribute for the object's visibility in the Channel Box. Right now its state shows *off*. But even if we set it to *on*, nothing would change. The attribute has to know what to do with *on*. We let Set Driven Key handle the communication between the new *rrringTheBell* attribute and the position of the knob. Set Driven Key will make the new attribute send out a command that causes the knob to snap forward.

1 Open the Set Driven Key window by choosing F2, Animate > Set Driven Key > Set ▢.
2 Load the attributes of the knob into the upper and lower fields (for the Driver and the Driven) of the window (see Figure 4.5).
3 In the upper-right field, mark the new *rrringTheBell* attribute.
4 In the lower-right field, mark the translation channel that is responsible for moving the knob into its pressed position. In the setup used here, it's *translate Y.*
5 Make sure that the knob is in its unpressed state and the new *rrringTheBell* attribute is set to off.
6 In the Set Driven Key window, click Key. From now on, whenever you set the new attribute to off, the knob will snap into its unpressed position.

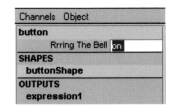

7 Move the knob into its pressed state.
8 In the Channel Box, type the word *on* into the field of the new attribute.
9 In the Set Driven Key window, click Key and close the window.

When you change the ringer attribute in the Channel Box from on to off, the ringer knob snaps back. We will now take care of the clapper itself.

1 Open the editor for the expression of the clapper. Complete the top of the previously created random expression by adding the following conditional statement (replace the attribute names with the ones you chose for your setup):

```
if
(button.rrringTheBell == 1)
ringerG.rotateY = rand (-0.5,0.5);
```

2 Click Edit to update the changes.

What this addition to the random expression says is *If* the attribute *rrringTheBell* is set to on (1 as opposed to 0), the bell will ring. It implies that if *rrringTheBell* is set to off, nothing will happen. The new attribute not only gives you control over the knob, it also lets you ring the doorbell.

If you handed the scene in this state over to your colleague busily animating a character who will occasionally ring the bell to get into the house, it would be much too complex. Your colleague would have to analyze the inner structure of your scene, see how Expressions and Set Driven Keys interconnect with objects and work on which attribute and so on. But we can make it so the next animator can focus on just one object : the red knob and its *rrringTheBell* attribute. The window for tidying up the Channel Box is called Channel Control.

1 Choose Window > General Editors to open the Channel Control window (Figure 4.6).
2 In its left field, mark all entries except the one for the ringer control.
3 Click Move to move the marked attributes to the Non Keyable section of the window and remove them from the Channel Box.

You can hide the attributes of all the other objects in the scene in the same way. Your colleague will open your scene, select the knob, and see only one attribute, which can be keyed when the character puts its giant thumb on the knob (Figure 4.7).

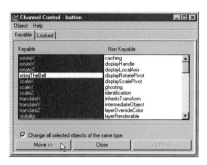

▲   *Figure 4.6 The left side of the Channel Control window lists all keyable attributes of the knob. All attributes but the new one are marked and will be moved to the right of the window. These attributes will then disappear from the Channel Box.*

▲   *Figure 4.7 After the tidying up, only one attribute is left in the Channel Box. That's all the character animator needs to see in order to make a character ring the bell.*

And now for something completely different: Ever looked at Incremental Save? Might save you a lot of pain!

WHICH WAY DID HE GO?

How do I make a character whiz away like in a cartoon?
Theme: Character Animation
Techniques and tools used: Jiggle Deformer, Graph Editor, Motion Blur

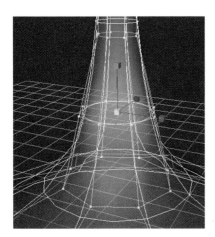

Figure 5.1 *The middle sections of the* ▲
Nurbs cone are scaled inward.

One of the key features of character animation is *anticipation*. Every step we take in real life has its phase of preparation. Before we swing a leg forward, we swing it back slightly—more forcefully when kicking a ball than while strolling through the park, but still we do it. This backswing is a movement in the reverse direction called *anticipation*. It has several characteristics, which we'll study in this tutorial using a simple object. The results can be used even for very subtle movements in order to enrich the personality of a complex 3D character. Cartoonists have always known about anticipation. When Donald Duck whizzes off from right to left we see him swing back slowly first before he whizzes out of sight within fractions of a second.

We'll use three very helpful tools for anticipation in this tutorial. The Jiggle Deformer (new in Maya 4) will make our figure sway back and forth sluggishly due to its inertia; the Graph Editor will give us precise control over the tangents of the keyframes; and rendering with Motion Blur will let us graphically stress the impression of speed.

1 Create a Nurbs cone. In the Channel Box, open the Inputs section and raise its Radius from 1 to 4 and its Spans to 4.
2 Select the three middle sections of the cone and scale them slightly inward toward the center axis (see Figure 5.1). Keep them selected.
3 Switch to animation (F2). Choose Animate > Create Jiggle Deformer to apply the Jiggle Deformer to the selected segments.

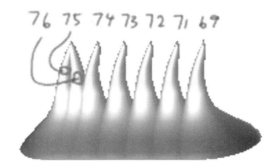

Jiggle deforms geometry based on motion data and inertia. No motion, no jiggle. So let's add some motion to our cone.

1 Prepare an animation range of 100 frames.
2 Go to frame 25 and select the cone.
3 Set a keyframe for its position using the command Shift+W.
4 Go to frame 75.
5 Move the cone 100 units to the left and set a second keyframe.

When you play back the animation, the top section of the cone (not the very tip and not the bottom of the cone, since we made only its middle soft) tilts after the cone starts moving (see Figure 5.2). Having reached its end position, the top still keeps swaying from inertia. The Jiggle Deformer brightens up this simple two-keyframe animation. But it has nothing to do with anticipation, so far.

Let's try an experiment:

1 Grab a pen from your desk and hold it still in front of you. Then move it very rapidly to the left. Accompany the movement with a whooshing-sound.
2 Repeat the procedure with a slightly different start: Give the pen a preliminary motion to the right before it whizzes away to the left. Accompany the movement with a cartoon sound as before.
3 Examine the timing of this motion: You intuitively begin with a long sound effect as you move the pen slowly to the right from its starting position. The pen slows even further and then immediately rushes off to the left with a short, sharp sound.

This motion sequence contains important clues about anticipation, which we'll now apply to our cone animation. The most important moment of anticipation is the turning point where the motion changes its direction, and where we'll now set a third keyframe. This point completes the anticipation

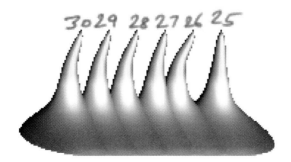

◀ *Figure 5.2 From frame 25 on, the cone starts moving from right to left. At frame 25 (far right) it stands up straight, at frame 26 it's accelerating strongly to the left and is therefore being deformed by the Jiggle Deformer. Although its motion is finished at frame 75 (far left), its top sways sluggishly back and forth for a while, due to inertia. Without the Jiggle Deformer this linear animation from right to left would be rather uninteresting.*

and occurs only fractions of a second before the whole animation ends. The preparation for whizzing away takes much longer than actually whizzing away (at least in a cartoon).

1 Go to the first keyframe of the cone.
2 In the Timeline, click and hold the middle mouse button while scrubbing forward to frame 70.
Using the middle mouse button in the Timeline lets you carry the frozen state of an animation from one point in time to another. The scene doesn't update. This way we don't have to find the cone and move it from its far away position at frame 70.
3 Move the cone to the right into its anticipation position.
4 Set a keyframe.

Now the cone leaves its original position moving slowly to the right for several frames and zips out of sight to the left within a few frames (see Figure 5.3). The Jiggle Deformer works hard at frame 70 where the direction changes. If the effect is too strong for you, open the cone's jiggle section in the Channel Box and raise the values for Stiffness and Damping.
We need to gain total control over the determining key at frame 70, so we'll now turn our attention to our cone's *tangents*—the graphic representation of how the animation approaches and leaves a keyframe.

Figure 5.3 Animation with cartoon-like anticipation. At frame 25 the cone starts moving slowly to the right. This preparatory motion in the opposite direction lasts about 2 seconds, until frame 70. Then all of a sudden our cone starts its movement to the left, reaching its end position as little as five frames later. It stops short, and the top keeps swaying for much longer. The strongest accelerations, and therefore the strongest jiggles, happen when the cone leaves the key of anticipation at frame 71 and after its sudden stop at frame 75. ▼

1 Select the cone and choose Window > Animation Editors to open the Graph Editor.
2 Ignore or delete all flat curves; they are not relevant for the animation.
3 Select the middle keyframe (at frame 70).
4 Click the Break tangents icon at the top of the window to break the animation's tangents at that key (see Figure 5.4).

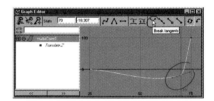

▲ *Figure 5.4 Here the animation runs too smoothly through the key of anticipation at frame 70, making it undramatic. To make the change of direction happen rapidly, we first need to break the tangents at this keyframe.*

5 Select the right part of the tangent and click the linear icon. This makes the tangent slope steeply in the direction of the last key.
6 Select the left part of the tangent and click the Flat tangents icon to lay it flat (see Figure 5.5).

The cone now moves slowly to the right, slows down even more before it reaches frame 70, and without warning whizzes off to the left, at a steep time curve. These two tangents give you fine control over the cone's anticipation. If you set the exiting tangent to flat as well, the cone wouldn't leave the turning point rapidly, but with a slight reluctance.

Rendering such an animation begs for motion blur. Motion blur is an effect from the world of real movie cameras that can easily be simulated by 3D software.

Before you render with motion blur, create a disk cache for the jiggle by choosing Deform > Jiggle Disk Cache. This tells Maya to save onto your hard drive the deformation data that the motion blur will use during rendering.

▲ *Figure 5.5 After setting the right tangent to linear—which in this case means steep and rapid—we set the left tangent to flat. Doing this makes the cone move very slowly to its turning point, but leave it rapidly and without warning.*

1 Open the Render Globals window.
2 In Render Globals, open the Motion Blur menu and select 2D for the Motion Blur Type (see Figure 5.6).
3 Render frame 71.

If the blur effect is too strong, reduce the Blur by Frame and Blur Length values in the Motion Blur menu.

If you want to render shadows, instead of 2D Motion Blur use 3D Motion

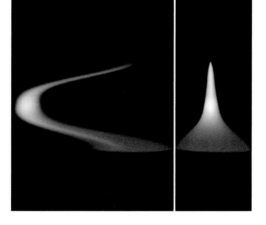

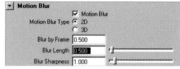

▲ *Figure 5.6 Activate 2D Motion Blur in the Render Globals window. You can reduce the blur values to make the effect less drastic.*

◄ *Figure 5.7 The cone, rendered with 2D Motion Blur to the right at the beginning and the left at the end of the animation.*

Blur. This requires higher antialiasing parameters and takes longer to render, but 3D Motion Blur creates shadows realistically blurred by motion . The 2D Motion Blur renderer doesn't blur the shadows (see Figure 5.7).

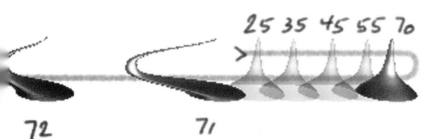

And now for something completely different: Ever tried leaving a little space below the Maya window, where minimized Maya window icons can jump into it?

SEMAPHORE FLAG SIGNALING

How can I animate semaphore signals?
Theme: Character Animation
Techniques and tools used: Joint Tool, Create Character,
Create Pose, Trax Editor, Create Blend

More than a century ago, semaphore flags were replaced by electric telegraph as the long-distance signaling system on land. To this day, however, ships still use semaphore for short-distance communication, and naval communications officers of yore used flags to convey messages of greeting, challenge, or deceit. In semaphore, each arrangement of the two flags represents a number or a letter. It is aesthetically pleasing to see a pair of arms waving the matched flags in a pattern that conveys information to a watcher who knows the system. In this tutorial, we'll send a semaphore message: the four letters M-A-Y-A. We'll use nonlinear animation to do it.

First, we need someone to hold the flags. In the front window, construct a simple skeleton consisting of a torso, two shoulders, and two arms.

1 Create a polygon plane and assign a ramp texture with two colors and sharp boarders to it (set Interpolation to None).
2 Rotate the texture using the Attribute Editor of its *place2dTexture* window. Set Rotate Frame to 45 degrees (see Figure 6.1).
3 Raise the Coverage of the texture to 2 x 2 and reduce the value of Translate Frame in V from *1* to *0.5*.

These settings create a diagonal composition of two colors.

4 Duplicate the plane by mirroring it on the Z-axis.
5 Parent the planes to their respective "hands."

In semaphore, the arms move like the hands of a clock (Figure 6.2). In order for the recipient of the message to determine when one word ends and the next begins, the alphabet contains a neutral position with both arms down. In this tutorial, we treat M-A-Y-A as a word where we want to stress every single letter and will therefore use the neutral position after each letter, and not only at the end. The various positions for each arm move from this neutral position 45 degrees at a time. The best tool to bring the arms into these positions is Rotation Snapping: Double-click the icon for rotation, activate Snapping, and enter a snapping value of 45.

From now on the rotation tool will click into place in increments of 45 degrees.

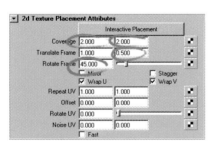

**Figure 6.1 The settings to place a ▲
ramp texture diagonally for the flag.**

Before nonlinear animation, we would have had to start animating the word M-A-Y-A with a keyframe in the neutral position. Then we would have rotated all participating joints into the position for the letter *M* and set a second keyframe, then rotated the joints back into their neutral position, set a keyframe, rotated to the letter *A,* keyframe, and so on. In fact, this is still the most straightforward way to animate just a single word. However, if you work, say, on a series of trailers for a scientific broadcast about the semaphore flag alphabet, and you have to signal lots of different words and sentences, it will save you a huge amount of time to use the keyframeless procedure laid out here.

Instead of setting keys, we create *poses* for each arm that cover all the various 45-degree positions—the whole alphabet. Creating these poses takes a bit of time, but once it's done the animation goes extremely smoothly. Whatever word you want to signal, just pick the relevant poses and arrange them in the Trax Editor.

In order to use poses in Maya we need to create *characters* from the participating objects. A character in this context has nothing to do with a 3D creature with a personality. A character in Maya is just a pool of different attributes of different objects. We have to create this pool before we can use these attributes in nonlinear animation. When we create a clip the character is generated automatically. Poses, however, require an extra little manual step. So we'll create two simple characters, one consisting of the Z-rotation of the left arm and flag, one of the Z-rotation of the right arm and flag.

1 Select the right flag (the left one as seen from the front) and the right arm. Reconfirm your selection in the Outliner: Make sure both the joint and the polygon plane are selected.
2 In the Channel Box, select Rotate Z.
3 Open the option window for creating a new character, by choosing F2, Character > Create Character Set (see Figure 6.3).

▲ *Figure 6.2 The letters and numbers of the semaphore flag system.*

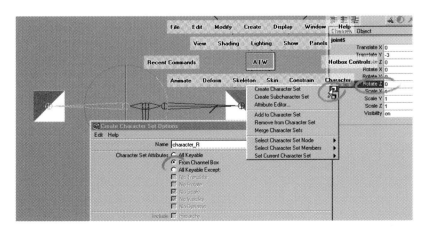

◄ *Figure 6.3 In order to convert the several positions of our flagbearer into poses, we first have to generate a new character—here for the right arm and flag.*

4   Check the option *From Channel Box*, give the character a name, and create it by clicking *Create*.

In the pop-up menu at the lower-right edge of the screen you see that the character has been created and is now active. That's all you need to know about it. We're ready for the poses of the right arm now.

1   Rotate the right arm so that it points straight down.
2   If necessary, rotate the corresponding flag; try to match the flag's position to the one in the semaphore alphabet.
3   For this neutral position create the first pose, by choosing Animate > Create Pose (see Figure 6.4). Give it an appropriate name.
4   Create further poses each of the 45-degree rotations of the right arm and its flag.

Figure 6.4 The first pose (neutral).   ▶

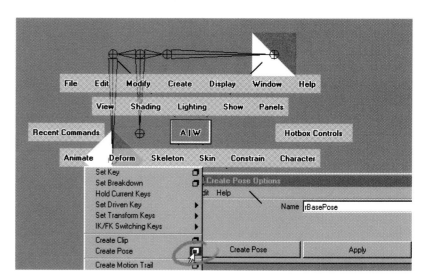

Use the picture of the semaphore alphabet as your guide. You don't have to select the objects you're creating poses for. As long as the character that contains the attributes in question is active, all keys you set are set for these parameters. This is the basic purpose and the greatest strength of using a character in Maya to assemble many parameters of several objects and make them easy to handle.

1   Open the Visor and try out the poses you created by right-clicking them and invoking Apply Pose (Figure 6.5).
2   Call up the poses of the right arm for the letters *M* and *Y*.
3   Rename them *M_r* and *Y_r*.

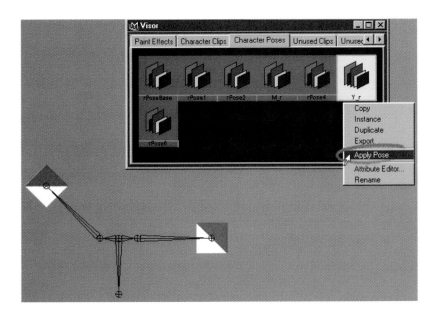

When signaling the letter *A*, the position of the right arm is in the same position as when signaling *M*.

1 Create a second character, this time for the Z-rotation of the left arm and the left flag.

2 Create poses for each of the 45-degree rotations of the left arm. The name you give to the first pose is being counted upward for all following new poses.

3 Try out the new poses using the Visor. Rename the pose for the letter *M* as *M_l*.

The left-arm pose for the letter *A* is the same as its neutral position, and the pose for *Y* shows the flag stretched out to the left as it does for the letter *M*.

You now have two sets of seven poses each for two different characters. When you activate a character in the pop-up menu at the lower right, you see the poses of that character in the Visor.

1 Open the Trax Editor by choosing Window > Animation Editors > Trax Editor.

This window is the control room for nonlinear animation. You may call it your Avid or Media 100 Editing Suite for 3D character animation. You find two entries here for the two characters.

2 Activate the right character using the pop-up menu at the lower right of the screen.

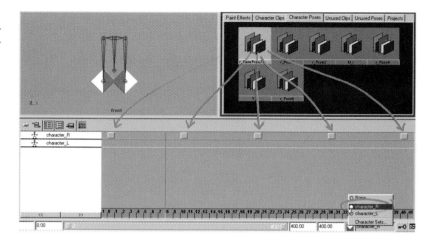

Figure 6.6 Using the middle mouse ▶
button to drag the neutral pose of the right
character from the Visor to five different
positions in the Trax Editor.

3   With the middle mouse button, drag the neutral pose of the right arm from the Visor to the upper track of the Trax Editor (see Figure 6.6).

You can navigate within the Trax Editor as in any other 2D window. Especially useful are the keys F for focusing on the selected object and A for focusing on all objects.

1   In the Trax Editor, move the neutral pose to frame 0 or 1.
2   Drag the neutral pose from the Visor to the Trax Editor four more times, to frames 10, 20, 30, and 40.
3   In the Visor, look up pose M_r and drag it to frame 5 in the Trax Editor.
4   Drag the same pose (which is also used for the letter *A*) to frames 15 and 35.
5   Drag the right-arm pose for *Y* to frame 25.

This was quick, and it goes equally fast with the second character, the left side of the signaler.

1   Select the character for the left side using the pop-up menu.
2   Drag the neutral pose from the Visor to the Trax Editor five times and position the bars just below the neutral poses of the right character (to frames 0, 10, 20, 30 and 40).
3   Drag the left-arm pose for *M*, M_l (which is the same as for *Y*), to frames 5 and 25.

Figure 6.7 The completed animation ▶
of the flags signaling M-A-Y-A—an
animation in the Trax Editor without a
single keyframe.

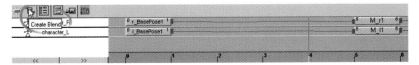

▲ *Figure 6.8 Smooth the transitions between one pose and the next using blends.*

When you scrub through the timeline you see that you created an animation without setting a single keyframe. At this point, the animation jumps from one pose to the next because Maya doesn't interpolate between them. You can blend between poses with just one click.

In the Trax Editor, select the first two neighboring poses and smooth in between by clicking the Create Blend icon (see Figure 6.8). Repeat this for the other pairs.

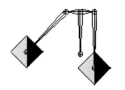

Now the animation plays back smoothly. You can see how smoothly in the Graph Editor, which opens as soon as you click its icon in the Trax Editor (see Figure 6.9). Select the blend lines and set their tangents flat in the Graph Editor, so they leave their previous positions and enter the next even more smoothly (see Figure 6.10).

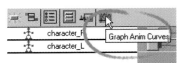

▲ *Figure 6.9 The fast way to get from the Trax Editor…*

The animation has a slight defect that can easily be fixed in the Trax Editor: The figure should hold the positions of the letters for a second before it continues to the next. Just drag the right end of the appropriate bars to extend them (see Figure 6.11). Reposition them slightly to the left and you're done. It's like working with editing software for digital video.

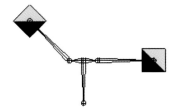

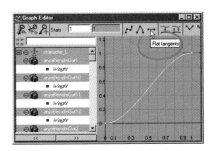

▲ *Figure 6.10 …to the Graph Editor, where you can edit the tangents.*

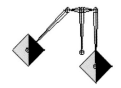

▲ *Figure 6.12 M-A-Y-A—our semaphore message is complete.*

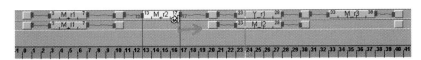

▲ *Figure 6.11 The poses for the letters are being stretched.*

And now for something completely different: Ever looked into the particle folders of past projects? And while you're at it, ever visited the depth folders?

Roll, Ball, Roll!

How do I get a sphere to roll, not scoot, over a hill?
Theme: Animation
Techniques and tools used: Make Live, Curve on Surface, Arc Measure Tool

It's trivial to move an object from left to right. It's easy to shove an object around on a flat plane. It's not so easy to shove an object over an uneven surface along a precise path (meaning you can't use dynamic simulation, which would produce slightly unpredictable results). If the object is a sphere that has to roll, not scoot, it calls for some thought. But let's postpone the thinking and start by shoving a cube along a path over a hilly surface.

1 Prepare an animation length of 400 frames.
2 Create a Nurbs plane with a Width of 20 and a density of 20 x 20 Patches in U and V.
3 Choose F3, Edit Nurbs > Sculpt Surfaces to deform the surface.
4 Select the surface and make it a "live" object either by clicking on the magnet icon at the top of the screen (see Figure 7.2) or by choosing Modify > Make Live. This means that from now on you can work directly on it.
5 Select one of the Create Curve tools and click or draw a curve across the whole surface.
6 Exit the Live mode by clicking the magnet icon again.

That curve you created right on the surface is the curve we want the cube to move along.

▲ *Figure 7.1 A (real) curve measurement device in the French Alps.*

▲ *Figure 7.2 The magnet icon at the very top of the Maya window lets you work directly on surfaces.*

▼ *Figure 7.3 Attach the cube to the curved surface.*

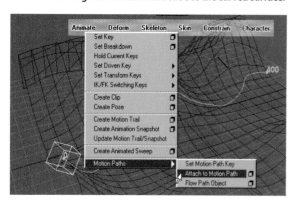

1 Create a polygon cube.
2 Press the 4 key to enter the wireframe mode. Select the cube, then the curved surface.
3 Create a motion path for the cube by choosing F2, Animate > Motion Paths > Attach to Motion Path (see Figure 7.3).

When you play back the animation you see the cube move along the curve up and down the hills. There's only one problem: Instead of moving on top of the surface, the cube sinks into it (see Figure 7.4).

This tendency to dip into the surface has to do with the cube's pivot. We could move the cube's pivot, but instead we'll delete the cube and create a Nurbs sphere. Let's talk

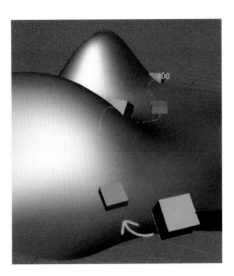

◀ *Figure 7.4 Our cube runs over (and dips into) the hills and through the valleys.*

about the sphere's pivot. If you attach the sphere to the path as you did earlier with the cube, its lower part will also dip into the surface. If you move the sphere's pivot down so that it doesn't sink, you can't rotate it around its center any more—and that's what you want to do in order to roll it (rather than scoot it) over the surface.

What we need here are two objects in one. One should follow the path, and the other should roll properly. The solution is hierarchic animation, a big word for the simple procedure of working with groups, members, and parents. All you have to do in this case is group the sphere with itself and attach the group to the path. The group's only member, the sphere, can then rotate around its center point while the group moves up and down the hills. The group takes the sphere with itself, and this sphere takes care of the rolling effect.

1 Group the sphere with itself using the keyboard shortcut Ctrl+G or by choosing Edit > Group.
2 Rename the group.
3 In Insert mode, move the *group's* pivot to the sphere's south pole (see Figure 7.5).
4 Attach the sphere's group—not the sphere itself!—to the curved surface just like you attached the cube before, by choosing F2, Animate > Motion Paths > Attach to Motion Path.

The sphere runs over (and not partly within) the surface (see Figure 7.6). In fact it's not the sphere that runs here, it's the sphere's group, which, of course, carries the sphere with itself wherever it goes. If the sphere in your setup tilts sideways to the path's curve, you can fix this by changing the internal axis of the motion path: Open the Attribute Editor of *motionPath1* and set its Up Axis to Y.

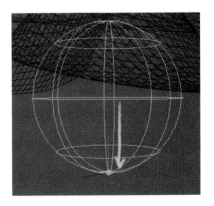

▲ *Figure 7.5 Moving the pivot of the sphere's group after grouping the sphere with itself. This makes the sphere stay on top of the surface as it moves along.*

Figure 7.6 Slippin' and slidin'—but ▶
not rollin'—over the hills.

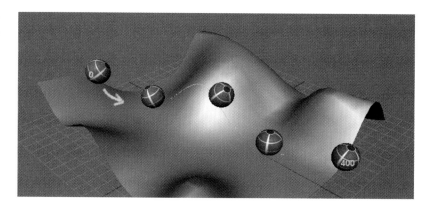

Now it's time to get rolling. How do we stop the sphere from just scooting? We make the sphere rotate within its group, to create the impression that it's rolling. If we divide the curve's length by the sphere's circumference we'll know how many times the sphere will have to turn around its axis on its way across the surface. The sphere's radius is 1. The formula for circumference is `2 * RADIUS * π`

So our sphere's circumference is `2 * 1 * 3.14 = 6.28`

So every time the sphere moves by a length of 6.28 units and performs exactly one rotation, it will look as if it actually feels the friction of the surface and rolls on it. Maya offers a couple of very useful ways to measure distances. The one we need for measuring the length of an irregular curve is the Arc Length Tool.

1 Choose Create > Arc Length Tool. In wireframe mode, click on the curve. The tool shows you the distance between the origin of the curve and the point you're clicking on (see Figure 7.7). Drag the Arc Length Tool to the end of the curve and note the value shown.

2 Divide the total curve length by the sphere's circumference, which is 6.28.

In the setup used here, the curve is 25.54 units long.
`25.54 / 6.28 = 4.07`

The sphere will therefore have to rotate approximately four times around its axis.

3 Multiply the result by 360.

Now you know how many degrees the sphere will have to rotate in order to roll along the whole path.

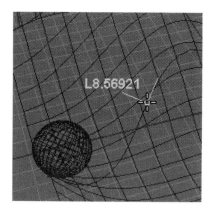

▲ *Figure 7.7 The Arc Length Tool*
measures the distance between the origin
of the curve and any point on the curve.

1 Go to the beginning of the animation.
2 Select the sphere (not its group!) and test which axis it turns on.
3 Set a keyframe for this rotation parameter.
4 Go to the end of the Timeline.

5 At frame 400, raise the rotation value by the number you just calculated and set another keyframe (see Figure 7.8).

6 Open the Graph Editor and set the tangents of the sphere's rotation curve to linear (see Figure 7.9).

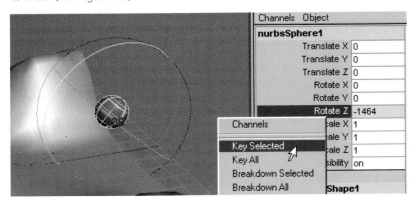

◄ *Figure 7.8 The rotation of the sphere receives its second keyframe after a little bit of calculation. In this setup it rotates by –1464 degrees around Z.*

If the sphere rotates in the opposite direction, reset the second keyframe, this time with a negative value. The animation will now show a sphere smoothly rolling along its winding path (see Figure 7.10).

This method gives you a convincing rolling motion in a very short time, but it is not very flexible. If, for example, a single parameter like the sphere's radius or the path's length changes, the rolling effect fails until you redo the calculation and reset the second keyframe. In order to control this you need to set expressions that use these parameters as variables.

There's another weakness to the animation in its current state: The sphere rolls along the path in a monotonous way; it doesn't accelerate when rolling downhill, for example. You can fix this by inserting more keyframes for the U Value of the motion path and the sphere's rotation. After which you will have to adjust the two animation curves in the Graph Editor.

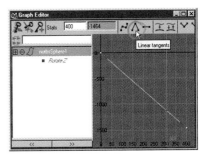

▲ *Figure 7.9 In order to create a convincing rolling motion the tangents have to be set to linear (if they weren't already).*

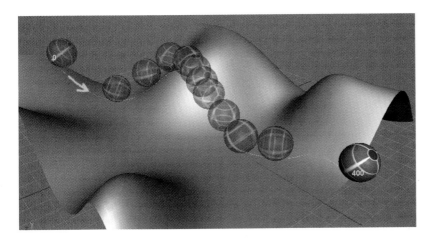

◄ *Figure 7.10 The sphere rolls convincingly along the winding road.*

And now for something completely different. Ever rendered a chain of rubies with Tom Kluysken's Caustics?

STEERING THE BIKE (WITH A LITTLE DISTRACTION)

How do I make a character steer a bicycle and in between draw an @-sign in the air?
Theme: Character Animation
Techniques and tools used: Joint Tool, IK Handle, Point Constraint, Motion Path

There's more to character animation than a digital figure's convincing facial play, authentic walking, and lip-synched speech. The figure also has to interact with the rest of its world. Although the questions raised in this context would in real life take many forms—touching, holding, releasing, looking, approaching—in computer animation they can be reduced to *Constraint*. The most important constraint is the one binding our character to another part of the world, whether an object or another character. In this tutorial, we'll cover the basic procedures for setting that kind of constraint. We'll animate a figure steering a bicycle and simultaneously drawing the @ sign in the air.

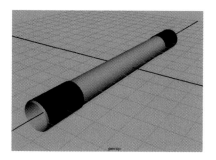

▲ *Figure 8.1 A bicycle's handlebar with grips made out of three Nurbs cylinders.*

1 Create a bicycle handlebar with two handgrips (see Figure 8.1). All you need are three cylinders, scaled accordingly. Leave the center of the handlebar in the origin of the scene. Group all three components together and give the group a meaningful name.

2 With the Joint Tool construct a skeletal shoulder and arm consisting of six or seven bones. Start with the neck, add a collarbone, and put in two more bones for the arm leading to the joint of the hand (see Figure 8.2).

Figure 8.2 Modeling a skeleton: ▶
With a few clicks in the appropriate windows, the left shoulder and arm are completed.

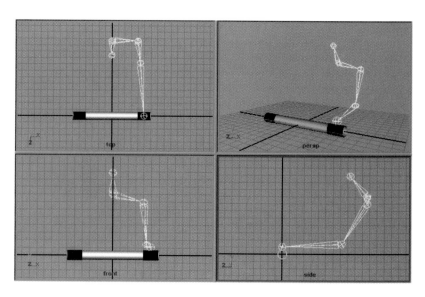

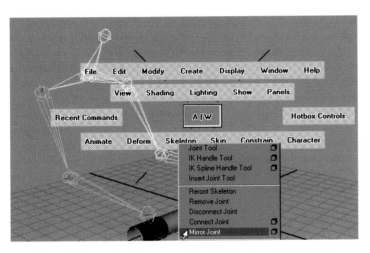

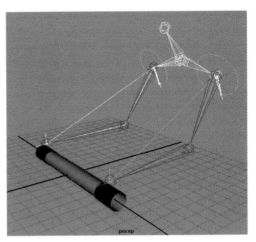

▲ *Figure 8.3 Then mirror the arm and shoulder to other side (here over the YZ plane).*

▲ *Figure 8.4 Two IK Handles make animating the arms easy.*

3 Now select the upper arm joint and mirror the whole assemblage over to the other side using the Mirror Joint command (see Figure 8.3). The neck is optional.
4 For both arms span IK Handles from the shoulder to the hand joints (see Figure 8.4).

Using the two IK Handles you can move the arms according to the laws of inverse kinematics. All you have to do is grab the IK Handle and move it to where you want, and the two bones of the arm will rotate accordingly and follow. We'll bind the IK Handles to the handlebar grips.

1 Select the right grip followed by the right IK Handle. Choose F2, Constrain > Point to constrain the IK Handle to the grip.

The right hand joint jumps to the center of the grip as soon as you set the constraint. We'll lift the hand again in a minute.

2 Use a Point Constraint to bind the left IK Handle to the left grip.
3 Select both grips and, in Insert mode, move their pivots upward so that the hand joints will be positioned slightly above the grips (see Figure 8.5).

Let's give the handlebar a little bit of motion.

1 Select the handlebar's group (which includes the grips). In the Outliner, click Rotate Z and use the context menu to call up the Expression Editor window.
2 Using the middle mouse button, copy the term next to Selected Obj & Attr and paste it into the empty Expression field (see Figure 8.6). Complete the entry with the function

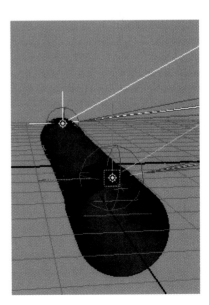

▲ *Figure 8.5 Moving the pivots of the grips upward lifts the hand joints.*

```
= SIN (TIME);
```

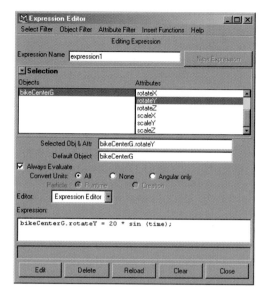

▲ *Figure 8.6 A mathematical equation makes the handlebars slalom.*

3 Create the new expression by clicking Create.

The sine function can take any input, in our case the number of seconds given by time. But sine's output can be only between –1 and +1. So when you watch the animation the handlebars rotate by only –1 to +1 degrees which of course is barely visible.

4 Edit the expression (you can call up the Expression Editor in the same way as before) by giving the sine function a 20-fold weight:

`= 20 * SIN (TIME);`

5 Accept the changes by clicking Edit.

This change gives the handlebar a leisurely rotation between –20 and +20 degrees around the Y-axis, just as if the bike were in a slalom. Since the point constraint is active, the arms move in concert with the grips. It looks just as if the arms (and not our expression) were steering (see Figure 8.7). If the arms in your setup are too short for the wider steering movements, don't make them longer—help them reach the grips by moving the shoulders or backbone slightly forward.

If you want to exclude one of the arms from the steering motion, try this: Click its IK Handle and in the Channel Box under Shapes set its Node State from Normal to Blocking (see Figure 8.8). This command makes the constraint inactive. You can key this attribute.

We will go one step further and instead of completely excluding the arm from steering, we'll add another constraint for the arm—a Locator. Then, rather than altering the constraint's Node State, we'll change its *weight*.

Figure 8.7 Both arms are steering, ▶
hands tight on the grips.

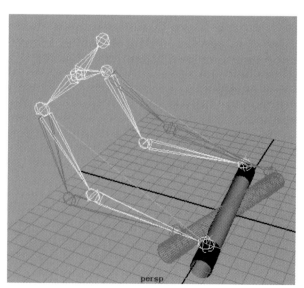

1 Create a Locator (an object which will not be rendered). You'll find it in the Create menu.
2 Move the locator into a position slightly to the right of the right arm.
3 With the locator still selected, select the right IK Handle and constrain it to the locator by choosing Constrain > Point.

The hand joint immediately reacts to this change and jumps to the midpoint between the grip and the locator. If you move the locator to another part of the scene, the IK handle follows sluggishly. The crucial parameters for this step are the Weights of the two constraints, which you'll find in the Channel Box right below the Node State. The first value is the weight of the grip, the second is the weight of the locator. Since both values are equal in our current setup, the hand finds a position exactly between them (see Figure 8.9).

1 Prepare an animation length of 1000 frames.
2 Go to frame 300. Set the weight of the right grip to *1* and the weighting of the locator to *0*.
3 Set keyframes for both parameters.
4 Move 50 frames ahead, to frame 350. Flip the weighting: 0 for the grip, 1 for the locator.
5 Again, set keyframes for both parameters.

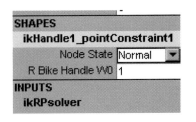

▲ *Figure 8.8 Switch the Node State from Normal to Blocking and the constraint becomes inactive so the arm can move around freely again.*

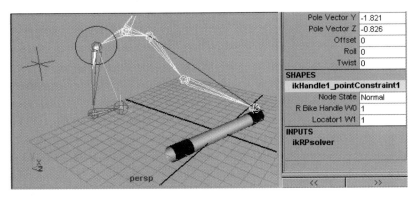

◀ *Figure 8.9 The weights W0 and W1 of the grip and the locator are equal. Therefore the hand joint positions itself between the two.*

By reversing the weight between the two point constraints you animated the motion of the arm. The hand separates from the handlebar at frame 300 and within 50 frames moves to the locator where it stays for the rest of the time.

6 Make the hand return to its grip between frames 500 and 600 by setting two more keyframes for the constraint weights.
7 Edit the animation in the Graph Editor to your taste. Set the tangents to flat where the motion starts and ends.

Between frames 350 and 500 the arm stays in one static position. If you animated the locator during this period, for example by giving it a waving

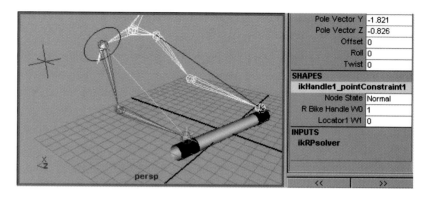

Figure 8.10 When the grip's weight ▶
is changed to W0 = 1 and the locator's
weight to W1 = 0 the hand joint jumps
back to the grip.

Pole Vector Y	-1.821
Pole Vector Z	-0.826
Offset	0
Roll	0
Twist	0
SHAPES	
ikHandle1_pointConstraint1	
Node State	Normal
R Bike Handle W0	1
Locator1 W1	0
INPUTS	
ikRPsolver	

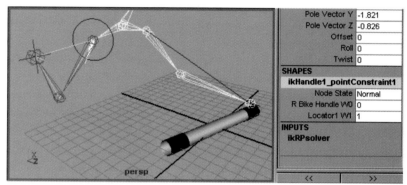

Figure 8.11 With settings W0 = 0 ▶
and W1 = 1, the hand joint jumps to
the locator.

Pole Vector Y	-1.821
Pole Vector Z	-0.826
Offset	0
Roll	0
Twist	0
SHAPES	
ikHandle1_pointConstraint1	
Node State	Normal
R Bike Handle W0	0
Locator1 W1	1
INPUTS	
ikRPsolver	

movement, the hand would be able to follow that movement because it's free from the influence of the grip. We let the hand do something concrete by having it draw the @ sign in the air. We achieve this with a further constraint that binds the locator (not the IK Handle this time) to the path of the sign.

1 Switch to the side or front view, and with the Pencil Curve Tool draw a free curve that describes the @ sign (see Figure 8.12).
2 Move the curve near the locator.
3 Select the locator, followed by the curve.

Figure 8.12 Drawing the @ sign ▶
in the side window.

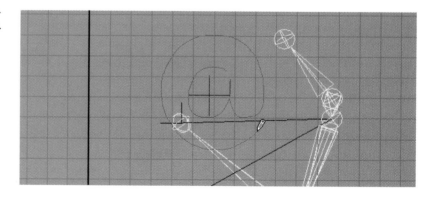

4 Open the option window of the Motion Path command by choosing Animate > Motion Paths > Attach to Motion Path ■.

5 In the Attach to Motion Path Options window, set the Time Range to Start/End. Set the Start Time to 400 and the End Time to 470 and apply the command by clicking Attach (Figure 8.13).

Now the hand moves away from the grip, draws the @ sign in the air, and finally returns to the grip and continues steering (Figure 8.14). Check the animation curves of the Motion Path in the Graph Editor to make sure the motions don't begin too rapidly. You can also set keyframe tangents to flat using the context menu of the Timeline.

If you construct a whole bicycle and cyclist, don't forget to pack the locator into one group with the rest of the assemblage. It might also be nice to add a little animation to the @ sign at this point. The shoulder could probably use a little bit of motion, too. How about a sine?

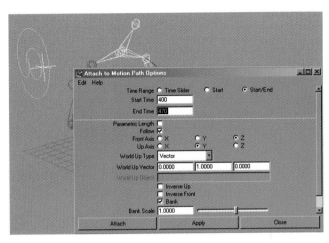

▲ **Figure 8.13 Between frames 400 and 470 the locator is being constrained to the path of the @ sign.**

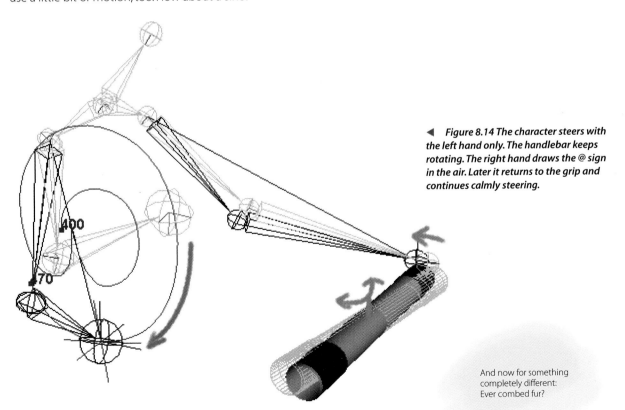

◄ **Figure 8.14 The character steers with the left hand only. The handlebar keeps rotating. The right hand draws the @ sign in the air. Later it returns to the grip and continues calmly steering.**

And now for something completely different: Ever combed fur?

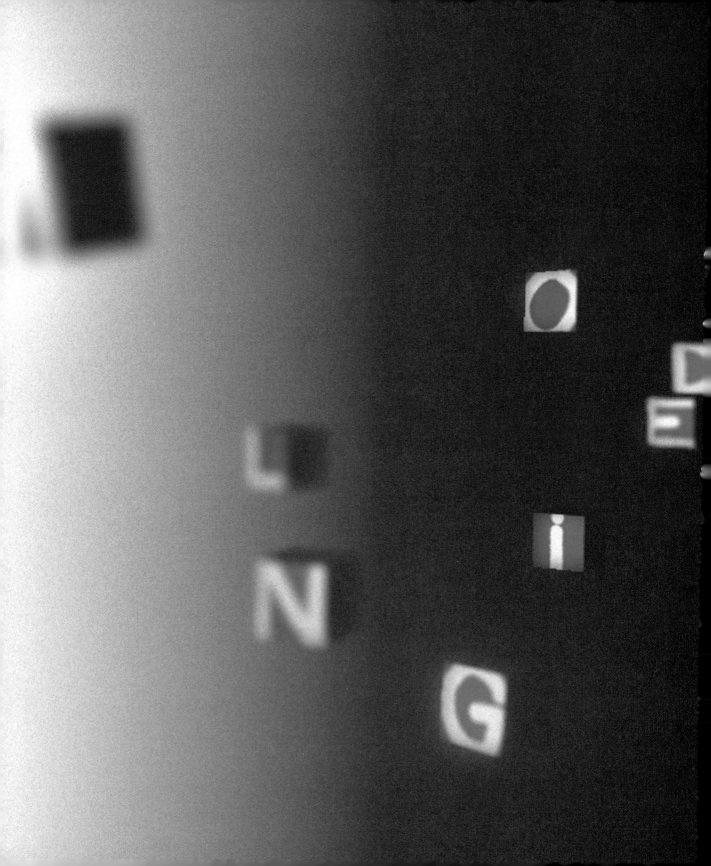

MODELING

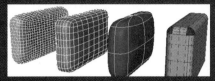

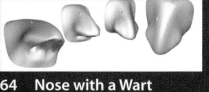

CABLE SPOOL

How do I coil a cable around a spool?
Theme: Modeling
Techniques and tools used : Animation Snapshot, Loft

In most projects, modeling and animation are two separate processes. There are, however, many objects that can be modeled much more easily by using animation instead of classic modeling tools. A roller blind for example, looked at from the side, reveals the shape of a snail's shell. If you model a roller blind starting from the profile (the spiral), it's too much effort. You get a very good result much more quickly by briefly thinking about how to create an *animation* along a spiral.

In this tutorial, we will model something similar: a cable coiled around a spool. The basic thought is this: We animate the cross-section of the cable—which is a circle—along the cable's path. If, in doing so, we create enough duplicates of that circle, we can make a loft over them all and have a completed cable. Fortunately, Maya offers a command that handles the job of duplication for us and at the same time lets us animate the coiling process.

1   Create a Nurbs circle.
2   Move it *5* units to the right in *X*, and halve its radius (see Figure 9.1).
3   In Insert mode, move its pivot back to the scene's origin.

If you rotate the circle around the Z axis now it performs a loop by itself. If you translate the small circle by one unit in Z for each complete loop, its

Figure 9.1 The pivot of the circle is ▶
moved back to the origin. With this
new rotation point we can prepare
the first coil.

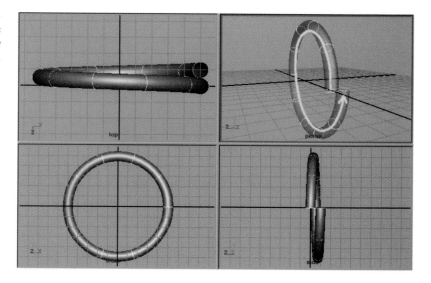

rotation path describes the first coil around the nonexistent spool (see Figure 9.2).

We'll establish ten coils for our cable. This requires a total rotation of 10 * 360° = 3,600° and a total translation to the right of 10 units. (If we choose a translation of more than 10 units, the cable won't coil compactly around the spool, but will have spaces between the coils—in certain cases a desirable effect.)

1 Establish an animation length of 100 frames.
2 Go to the beginning of the animation. Set keyframes for the circle's Translate Z and Rotate Z in their starting positions and rotations.
3 Go to the end of the animation. In the Channel Box, change Translate Z to –10 and Rotate Z to 3600. Set keyframes for these parameters (see Figure 9.3).
4 Open the Graph Editor. Set the animation curves to linear (see Figure 9.4).

Linear tangents are necessary to get a uniform coil. If you had flat tangents, the coiling would accelerate at the beginning and slow down towards the end, providing too high a density of circles for the loft there.

1 Select the circle.
2 Open the option box of F3, Animate > Create Animation Snapshot ❒.
3 Set the Time Range to Time Slider.
4 Apply the command by clicking Snapshot.

Animation Snapshot delivers 100 or 101 circles—depending on whether your animation starts at frame 0 or 1—which describe the coiling around the spool.

1 Select all the circles with a selection rectangle (see Figure 9.5).

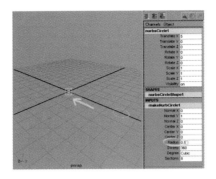

◀ *Figure 9.2 If we rotate the little circle by 360° around the Z axis and at the same time translate it by one grid unit in Z, we can visualize the first coil around the spool.*

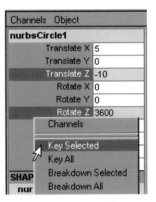

▲ *Figure 9.3 The translation and rotation channels of the circle receive keyframes at frame 100.*

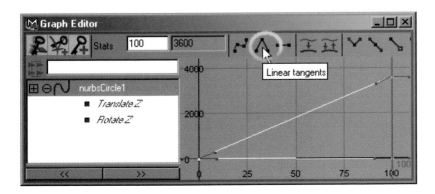

◀ *Figure 9.4 In order to achieve a uniform coil, we need a linear animation, instead of one that starts and ends slowly. So we set the tangents of the animation curves to linear.*

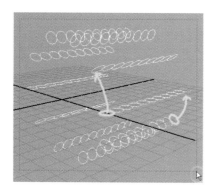

▲ *Figure 9.5 A large selection rectangle prepares for the loft across all 101 circles. The yellow arrows indicate the first and last circles provided by the Snapshot tool.*

Note that the last circle is shown in green, indicating that it's the last item selected. For the next step—creating the loft surface over all the circles—the selection sequence is important. In our case, we don't have to care about it since the selection rectangle automatically presents us with the right sequence: circle 1, circle 2, circle 3, and so on up to the last circle.

We said at the outset that we wanted to *model*, rather than animate our coil. So with this last command, we'll return to modeling.

2 With all circles selected, choose F3, Surfaces > Loft (see Figure 9.6).

If the loft surface looks blocky instead of round, press the 3 key in order to get a better display. The last circle contains all the information about the snapshot.

1 Select the last circle.
2 In the Channel Box, open the section *snapshot1* (see Figure 9.7).

Here you'll find the generation history of the surface, and by animating the Start and End Time you can animate how the cable coils around the spool. With a Start Time of 0 and an End Time keyed from 0 to100, the cable

Figure 9.6 The lofted surface across ▶ *all 101 circles represents 10 perfect coils around an as yet nonexistent spool.*

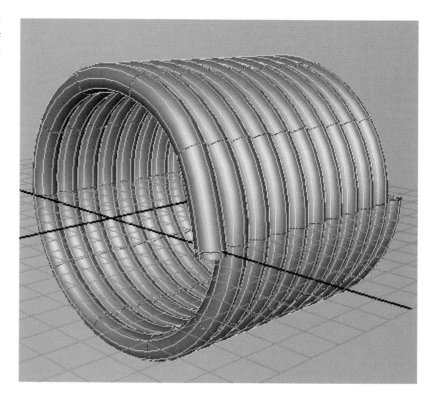

eventually coils over the drum. By animating the Start Time you make the cable decrease in length from the back (see Figure 9.8).

When the cable is coiled to your satisfaction, you can add the finishing touches. A simple cylinder, maybe with a few scalings where the caps are, will serve as the geometry for the spool. You might also want to play with a wood texture which you find in the 3D-texture-Section of the Hypershader (see Figure 9.9).

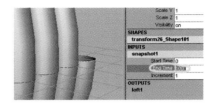

▲ *Figure 9.7 The cable with different settings for the End Time of the loft.*

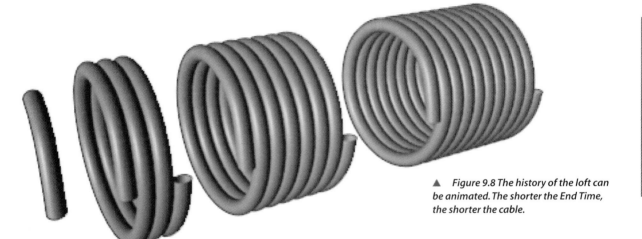

▲ *Figure 9.8 The history of the loft can be animated. The shorter the End Time, the shorter the cable.*

◄ *Figure 9.9 Coil a copper material around the cable and add a cylindrical assemblage with a wood texture to serve as the spool.*

And now for something completely different: Ever clicked a horse into your scene using Bert van Brandes' SkeletonWorks.

10

KNOBBLY MAN

How do I construct a figure whose surface is rougher than the usual 3D character's?
Theme: Modeling, Rendering
Techniques and tools used: Subdivision Surfaces, Split Polygon Tool, Extrude Faces, Displacement Shader

Most 3D objects have flawlessly smooth surfaces, which makes them too perfect for certain contexts. The usual procedure for giving a surface a little bit of roughness is to fake deformations using so-called Bump Maps. In fact, the Bump Map isn't a feature of the surface itself, it is a feature of the camera. Most of the time, Bump Mapping is sufficient and it's very economical in terms of rendering time. It fails, however, when you need very pronounced deformations and bulges that contrast sharply with the background.

Enter Displacement Mapping—a technique that doesn't fake the deformation for the camera but actually deforms the surface using the gray tones of a procedural texture or a picture. Unfortunately, we don't see these deformations in the modeling views. We have to render them.

This tutorial consists of two parts that fit together nicely. We start by using subdivision surfaces to model a tall, thin man with a small head. With a little bit of practice this task takes only a few minutes. (Before the era of subdivisions it was a matter of at least an hour.) If you don't have Maya Unlimited you can achieve similar results by using the same split and extrude tools and applying the Polygons > Smooth operation at the very end. If you want to skip the modeling part or keep it for later, just use any kind of primitive and continue with the displacement part of this tutorial.

1 Create a polygon cube.
2 Choose Modify > Convert > Polygons to Subdiv to convert the cube into a subdivision surface.
3 Assign a new material to the subdivision cube.

If you inadvertently textured the cube (which is actually just the outer skin of the subdivision surface and not the surface itself) instead of the subdivision surface, undo the assignment. Select the actual subdivision surface *polyToSubdShape1* (for example, in the Hypergraph) before you assign the material again. For the following actions, right-click the subdivision object and use the context menu.

4 Switch to Polygon mode (see Figure 10.1).

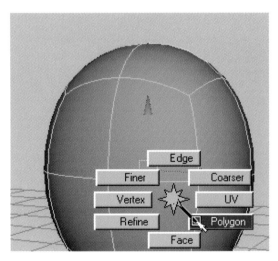

Figure 10.1 A polygon cube converted ▲
into a subdivision surface. Its context
menu allows us to make the original
polygon visible.

You can model with subdivision surfaces in two general modes. One is using the polygon tools, the other is using tools from the world of Nurbs modeling. The classic polygon modeling tools are ideal for achieving higher geometric resolution (for example, in the area where the legs come out of the torso). That's why we'll perform most of the modeling for our guy in Polygon mode.

1   Choose Edit Polygons > Split Polygon Tool to break the cube's bottom face in two (see Figure 10.2). Just eye it, don't try to be too precise—our character isn't going to enter a beauty contest. Finish the Split command by pressing Enter.

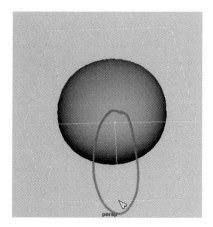

▲   *Figure 10.2 Use the Split Polygon Tool to split the lower face of the cube into two parts.*

▲   *Figure 10.3 The Extrude Tool creates a locally higher density of geometry. Here we use this density to start pulling out faces for modeling the legs.*

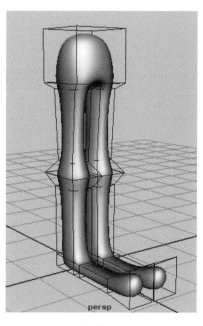

▲   *Figure 10.6 The lower extremities are completed—with a little practice it takes only a couple of minutes.*

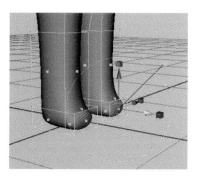

▲   *Figure 10.4 A few extrudes later and the legs are finished—not at all perfect, but they're legs. The last extrudes (horizontal this time) will make the feet.*

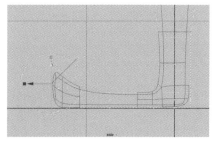

▲   *Figure 10.5 View from the side for more precise modeling of the ends of the feet.*

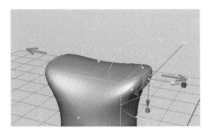

▲ *Figure 10.7 Working the upper body: Here are the first two extrudes for the arms.*

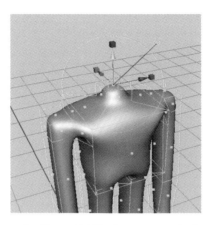

▲ *Figure 10.8 The first two extrudes for the neck and head.*

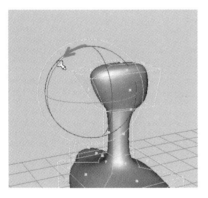

▲ *Figure 10.9 Aftermath: rotation of the back of the head.*

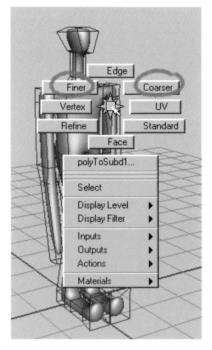

▲ *Figure 10.10 The context menu of the subdivision surface lets you switch between different levels of hierarchy. Finer levels let you work more locally.*

2 Use the context menu to make the Faces visible. Select the newly created two bottom faces of the cube. Choose Edit Polygons > Extrude Face to pull new geometry out of these faces (see Figure 10.3). Clicking on one of the scaling cubes of the tool puts the tool into scaling mode. Homogeneously scale down the extruded surfaces a little. Use the tool's arrow to translate them down a bit.

3 Don't lose your selection, press the G key to apply the extrude command again, this time to the freshly extruded faces. Pull the legs out of the torso by applying the command two or three more times. With the last extrude, create faces of a size that can be used to pull the feet out to the front (see Figure 10.4).

4 When extruding and scaling the feet, use the side and top views to work more precisely (see Figure 10.5).

1 Use the Split Polygon Tool on the sides of the torso and start extruding the arms (and, if you like, fingers). The extrude command works symmetrically, so you can extrude geometry simultaneously for the right and left arms (see Figure 10.7).

2 Extrude the top face of the subdivision polygon, scale down the cross-section of the neck and start pulling out the neck and head (see Figure 10.8).

3 Check the whole figure, adjusting faces to your taste. Keep in mind that you don't have to just translate and scale, you can also rotate faces (see Figure 10.9)!

In the Channel Box, you can see that after all the extrudes you've done the surface's construction history contains a lot of information we don't need any more. Deleting history using the Edit > Delete by Type > History command also makes the scene a little lighter.

What you *don't* delete by deleting the surface's history is its identity as a subdivision surface. By using the context menu and the commands Coarser and Finer, you can switch from one level of hierarchy to the next in order to work more globally or locally, in polygon as well as in standard mode (see Figure 10.10).

You don't need to add too much detail to your fellow at this point, like a nose, shoulder blades, or toes. The Displacement Shader might wipe away features as small as a nose or shoulder blades anyway.

1   In the Attribute Editor of the surface's shading group (in the case of a Blinn shader, its name will be *blinn1SG*), click the checker icon next to Displacement Mat.

2   The Create Render Node window opens (see Figure 10.11). Chose a texture here that will deform the character according to its gray values, such as the Solid Fractal. For the mapping method, select "As projection." The projection will make sure that the texture is distributed evenly over the whole object.

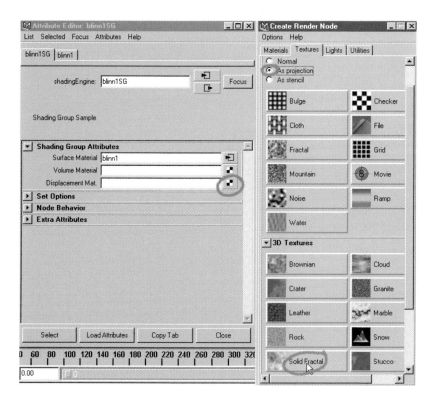

◄   *Figure 10.11 This is how to create a Displacement Map of a 3D texture by projection: Open the Attribute Editor of the Shading Group, click the checker icon next to Displacement Mat., and in the Create Render Node window choose "As projection" for the method and, for example, Solid Fractal as its structure.*

Figure 10.12 These two characters ▶
possess the same geometry and the same texture; the only difference is the way the texture was applied. The unevenness of the front figure comes from a Bump Map, whereas the back figure's texture is a Displacement Map. The edges of the front figure look smooth, but the Displacement Mapping on the other creates real bulges. Although no extra tuning was applied to the mapping procedure, the Displacement Map thickens the character drastically whereas the Bump figure basically shows the original size of the modeled geometry.

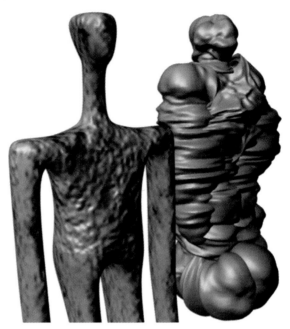

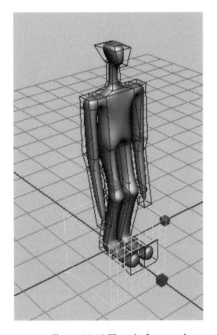

● Since you'll see no change in the modeling view, render the scene.

Rendering takes a while, maybe several minutes, depending on the geometry and material used and, of course, the speed of your computer. The results really clarify the difference between Displacement Mapping and Bump Mapping. In Figure 10.12, the character in the front was assigned the same Solid

▲ *Figure 10.13 The wireframe cube at the character's feet determines the dimension of the Displacement Map. The smaller that cube, the more frequently the texture is repeated on the object.*

Figure 10.14 The 3D placement ▶
object now covers the whole character. To the left is the rendered scene. With the marked icon you can save rendered pictures to memory. They won't be deleted until you exit Maya (or until the program crashes).

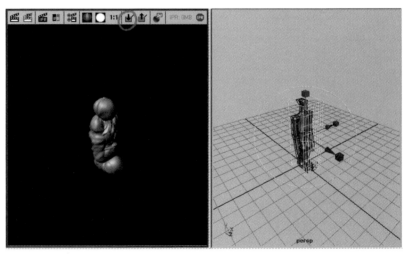

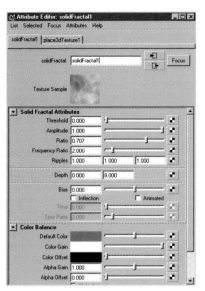

◀ *Figure 10.15 The texture's Attribute Editor. In the upper area are the parameters responsible for the structure of the fractal, lower down are the settings for gray, which are responsible for the amount of deformation. The main parameters when dealing with a Displacement Map are Color Gain and Alpha Gain. Higher values mean more white, which leads to an enlarged figure. When the Displacement Map finds only black it leaves the geometry untouched.*

Figure 10.16 A character ▶
that looks sculpted from clay.

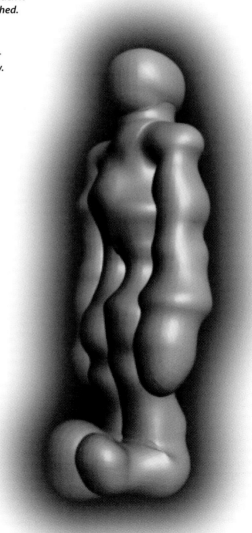

Fractal texture as the character in the back, but the texture was assigned as a Bump Map rather than as a Displacement Map (as for the character in the back). The surface of the front figure looks uneven, but its edges look totally smooth against the background.

Displacement Mapping has more or less effect, depending on how large you constructed your knobbly figure. There are two ways to adjust the strength of the effect. One is by changing the density at which the texture is mapped onto the geometry. In the modeling views you can see a wireframe cube named *place3dTexture1;* that's the tool that lets us make these changes (see Figure 10.13).

The second way to adjust the displacement texture is by using the texture's gray values. Displacement Mapping, like Bump Mapping, makes use of only the brightness (the alpha channel, not the color) of a texture in order to create geometric deformations. For most textures, such as the Solid Fractal, you'll find the grayscale entries under the Color Balance section in the Attribute Editor. First start with very dark, almost black values for the colors and a very low value for the Alpha Gain (see Figure 10.15).

Basically you let the character grow in size by applying a bright texture. A Displacement Mapping that finds only black will leave the figure unchanged. If the texture shows areas of distinct changes in brightness, the character will look very bulgy, with the bright areas of the texture corresponding to the bulges on the surface.

You'll have to use a lot of trial and error to find a proper combination of settings to achieve the result you have in mind. Unfortunately, IPR doesn't work with Displacement Maps, which means you have to deal with extended periods of test rendering. Use the render window's option to render smaller sizes or only parts of pictures.

With subdivision modeling and Displacement Mapping you have two strong tools for efficiently creating complex characters that look like they're made of clay (see Figure 10.16) or maybe hammered from metal (see Figure 10.17). To create a finer texture, you might add a Bump Map in addition to the Displacement Map. The bumps can then work as tiny deformations on the larger deformations.

The modeling process leaves your character with very unevenly distributed UV texture coordinates. You would see this if you had used Normal rather than Projection as your method of mapping. In order to fix these texture distribution problems you need to create a new UV texture map, for example by applying the command Automatic Mapping, which you'll find in the Subdiv Surfaces menu.

A projected texture like the one we're dealing with here doesn't care about UV coordinates. But as soon as you start animating the character, you'll have to bake the projected texture onto the geometry. Otherwise it will look as if when the character moves it's swimming through the texture. You find the command for baking textures in the Hypershader: Choose Edit > Convert to File Texture. If you want to use the sophisticated tools for polygon texture mapping, save your scene and then convert the subdivision creature into a polygon creature (choose Modify > Convert > Subdiv to Polygons).

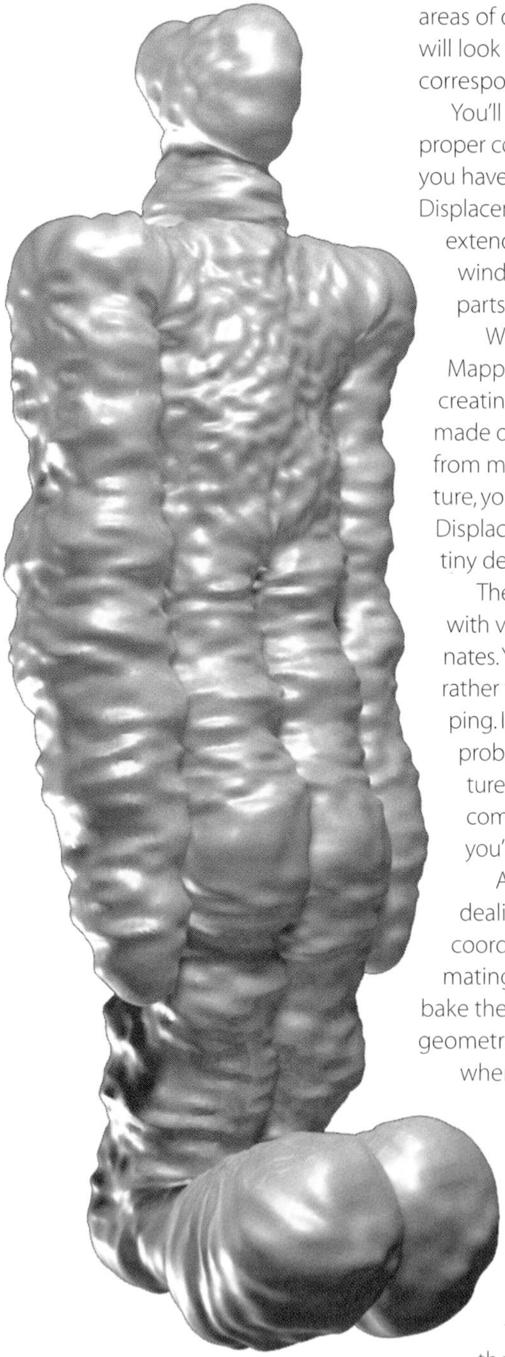

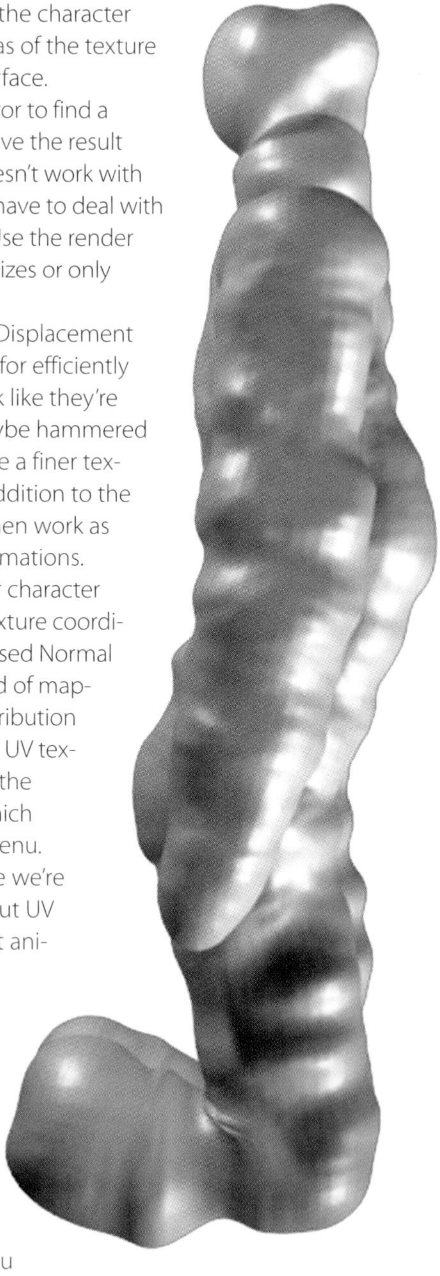

Figure 10.17 ▲
Hammered-metal knobbly guys.

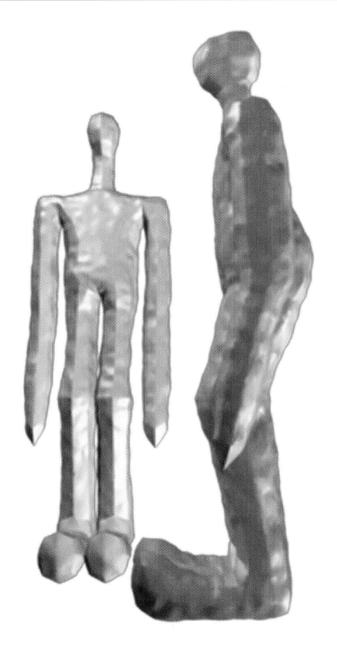

◀ *Figure 10.18 Knobbly guys hammered out of gold.*

And now for something completely different: Pressed the A or F key recently?

11

FENDER BENDER

How can I construct a car's fender from a few good Nurbs curves?
Theme: Modeling
Techniques and tools used: Loft, Square, Birail

When cars are designed the fenders (the part that curves over the wheels) are only very rarely designed separately. The fender shape is subject to the overall appearance of the car and is usually part of the whole design process. Nevertheless, the fender is a good exercise in creating a very specific shape by using specific curves.

In this tutorial, we will continuously create and modify curves, then create surfaces from them which we'll evaluate and delete. We'll start with only two curves that will form a loft, next we'll use the Square tool, and we'll end with the Birail 3+ Tool. That delivers a surface based on two rail curves and several profile curves, and that's the only surface we'll actually keep. Starting off with the highest tool is often not the best way. The first simple loft will already provide us with excellent curves for better surfaces.

1 In the front window, use the EP Curve Tool and with about eight clicks create a straight curve along the X axis.

2 Duplicate the curve and move the duplicate up.

3 Choose F3, Surfaces > Loft to create a surface from the two curves.

4 In the pick mask, uncheck *surfaces* so from now on you can only select curves (see Figure 11.1). You can, of course, still select the surfaces in the Outliner.

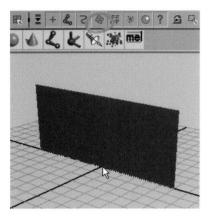

▲ *Figure 11.1 A lofted surface between two parallel curves. In the pick mask at the top of the screen, the surfaces are deactivated. In this mode, when you're working on curves, you won't inadvertently select the surface.*

Figure 11.2 The top of the wheel ▶
well gets its shape from the Proportional Modification Tool. It has a stronger effect on the CVs in the middle than on the CVs at the edge of the selection.

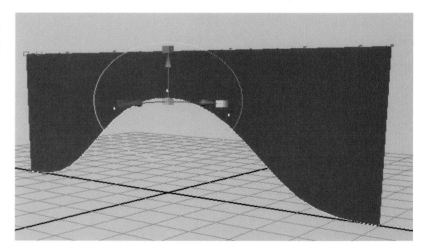

5 Choose Modify > Transformation Tools > Proportional Modification Tool to move the middle CVs of the lower curve upwards. They shape the entrance to the wheel well (see Figure 11.2).

6 Scale the CVs of both curves to the left and right of the wheel well inward to make this area smaller (see Figure 11.3). Remember not to move CVs across each other.

7 Translate the front CVs of both curves in the Z direction to give the fender a slight rounding toward the (nonexistent) radiator grille on the car's front (see Figure 11.4).

8 Translate the top CVs (except the ones you just moved) slightly in the Z direction to bend the fender toward the hood (see Figure 11.5).

9 Translate the front CVs of the upper curve slightly back to indicate the slope of the car's front (see Figure 11.6).

▲ *Figure 11.3 The Proportional Modification Tool is not only good for translating CVs, it's also good for scaling CVs. Here we make the entrance to the wheel well slightly smaller and rounder. The corresponding CVs of the upper curves should be scaled accordingly, in order to keep the geometry of the surface clean.*

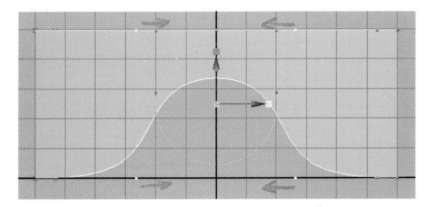

◄ *Figure 11.4 Both front CVs are moved to the right to suggest the front of the fender rounding toward the radiator grille.*

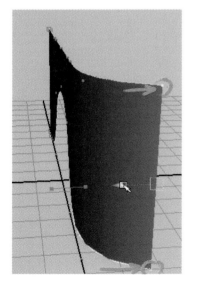

◄ *Figure 11.5 By slightly translating the remaining top CVs, the side of the fender gets a sloping shape toward the hood (left).*

◄ *Figure 11.6 The top front CVs are moved back to give the front of the car a slope (right).*

Your fender looks far from perfect. But consider how little time you've spent on it so far! The fender already looks like a fender and nothing else. However, after these few manipulations of curves, you'll encounter the restrictions of using lofted surfaces. The horizontal curves give you good control over the basic shape, but you lack vertical control; you need curves that allow you to insert distinctive marks such as a sharp edge just above the opening of the wheel well. Also, both vertical edges of the surface are absolutely straight, but they should actually show a smooth rounding. You could insert a third curve between the two existing curves and create a new loft to achieve this rounding, but this would be a very indirect way of doing it. You can gain absolute vertical control over the surface only with vertical curves.

In the next part, we'll use the Square tool, which will give us a surface made of four boundary curves that touch or intersect each other. If this tool isn't available in your version of Maya, use the Birail 2 Tool.

Before deleting the lofted surface, select it and take a last look at its construction, its parametrization. The loft consists of two horizontal and a few almost parallel vertical curves. If any of the isoparms (the curves that construct the surface) run across each other, something is wrong with your curves and you should rebuild them (see Figure 11.7).

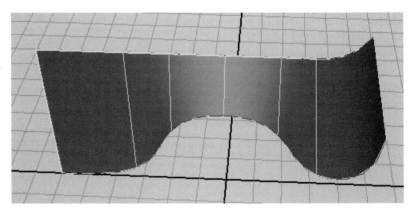

▲   *Figure 11.7 A basic fender shape, consisting of several vertical and two horizontal curves.*

1 Delete the lofted surface.
2 With the EP Curve Tool and just two clicks (each), create two new curves that connect the two horizontal curves (see Figure 11.8).

It is important that you use Curve Snapping (press and hold the C key) when creating the new vertical curves. This is the only way to ensure that the curves actually meet. Two clicks per curve (one at the top, one at the bottom) are sufficient. Pay attention to the direction of the curves. They should be identical.

3 Select the four curves clockwise or counterclockwise and use the command Surfaces > Square to create a new surface. The construction of the surface will fail if the curves don't meet.

The new surface looks similar to the lofted surface we had before, but now you can influence the fender's vertical shape.

4 Move both middle CVs of the rear curve (the one toward the back of the car) horizontally to round the edge of the fender.

5 Move both middle CVs of the front curve (the one toward the radiator) slightly forward to give the already sloped front of the fender a little bit of rounding as well (see Figure 11.9).

Note how powerful these tiny changes of curvature are and how they influence the whole structure of the surface. If you feel like moving CVs at the ends of any curves, be sure you also pick and move the corresponding CVs of the touching curves—otherwise the square surface cannot be generated any more. It's also a good idea to move the corresponding CVs of opposite curves together, since single-sided changes can have an unpredictable effect on the flow of the isoparms. After you delete the surface, the four remaining curves describe the shape of a fender much better than the curves that were left when you deleted the loft (see Figure 11.10).

1 Delete the square surface.

2 Go to the front view.

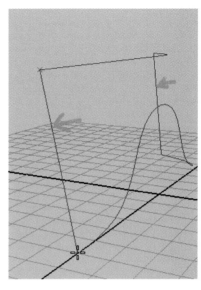

▲ *Figure 11.8 Two new curves with two clicks each. They connect the ends of the previous curves.*

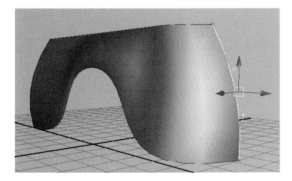

▲ *Figure 11.9 A new surface made out of four curves. Moving the two middle CVs of the front curve makes the front of the car round.*

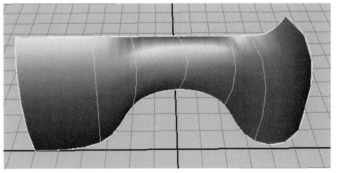

▲ *Figure 11.10 The end of the second phase of prototype design: the square surface before it's deleted.*

3 Create two new vertical curves running from the entrance of the wheel well up to the top curve (see Figure 11.11). Again, use Curve Snapping and only two clicks each.

Figure 11.11 Two new vertical curves created ▶
with the EP Curve Tool and Curve Snapping.

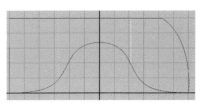

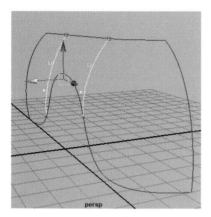

**Figure 11.12 Move the middle CVs ▲
out horizontally (to the left) to give the
middle of the fender a rounded shape.**

4 Switch to the perspective view. Translate the two middle CVs of the two
new curves in *Z* to align them with the other vertical curves (see Figure 11.12).
5 Deselect all curves.
6 Call up the Birail 3+ Tool by choosing Surfaces > Birail > Birail 3+ Tool.

As you might guess from the name, this tool gives us a surface from two
(bi) curves *(rail)*; the 3+ part means that we're using three or more *profile*
curves between the rails. In our case, the rails are the two original horizontal
curves, held together (profiles) by the four vertical curves. The help line at the
lower-left of the screen shows you the way. It asks you to pick the profile
curves first.

7 Select the four vertical curves and press Enter.
8 Select the two horizontal curves and press Enter.

This creates a new surface—our last one (see Figure 11.13). It looks quite
different from the previous surfaces. Around the new vertical curves we see
several isoparms, which makes the whole surface shape less elegant. This will
change soon.

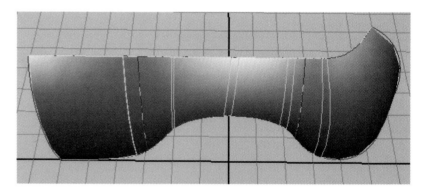

▲   *Figure 11.13 The birail surface looks less tidy than the previous surfaces because it
has to take into account additional curves in its center.*

We introduced the middle profile curves in order to prepare for a more
detailed structure that many cars show just above the wheel well. The CVs
of the vertical curves are not sufficient at this point to create this much detail.
If you open the curves' Attribute Editor you'll see that they are made out of
only a single span, meaning two clicks with two CVs in between. We need to
rebuild the curves to give them more CVs. In order to keep the geometry
clean we'll rebuild all four vertical curves in the same way.

1 Select all four vertical curves.
2 Choose Edit Curves > Rebuild Curve to open the option box ▢. Set the
Number of Spans to 4 (see Figure 11.14). Complete the command by clicking
Rebuild.

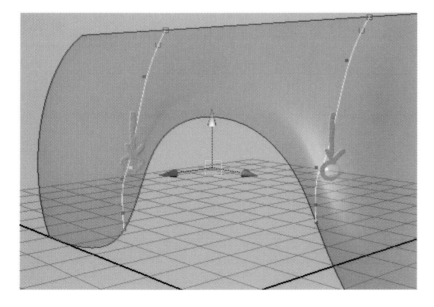

◀ *Figure 11.14 Reconstructing all profile curves, so we can add more detail above the wheel well and create a characteristic sharp edge.*

When all the vertical curves have been rebuilt the birail surface shows a higher density of horizontal patches. Note that the surface doesn't have to be rebuilt, it instantly adapts to the new curve attributes.

3 In component mode (F8), make visible all CVs of both middle vertical curves (the last curves you created).
4 For both curves select the fourth CV counting from the bottom (see Figure 11.15).
5 Move these two CVs down slightly.

A magic moment: This minimal translation of the proper relevant CVs creates the desired edge just above the wheel well. A nice feature of this edge is that it fades out smoothly to the front and back, just like on a real car. This smoothness is due to the interaction between neighboring vertical curves.

◀ *Figure 11.15 Translating precisely picked CVs on both curves slightly downward creates the characteristic edge above the wheel well. This edge fades in and out smoothly to the front and back since the CVs of the front and back curves are still equally distributed.*

Figure 11.16 Many more isoparms ▶
shape the rebuilt surface.

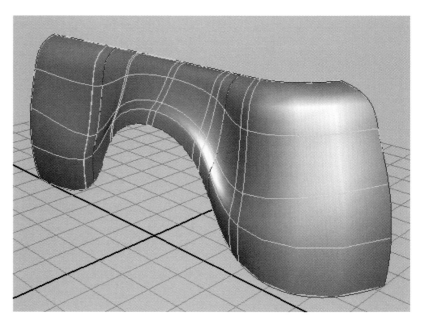

With this additional geometry you now can add detail to the top of all vertical curves (see Figure 11.16). Try to move the corresponding CVs of the curves together if possible. Check—maybe in another window with another shading mode—what impact the curve manipulations have on the flow of isoparms and surface patches.

If there aren't enough CVs to model as you wish, reconstruct the curves again. When you're satisfied, reconstruct the whole surface. Doing this will distribute the isoparms evenly.

1 Open the surface's Attribute Editor and note both the U and V values of Number of Spans.

Let's suppose the values are 17 and 4, meaning 17 vertical and 4 horizontal isoparms. For a sophisticated surface, 4 is a small number and should not be reduced further. However, 17 is more than we need at this point of modeling and can be reduced by about half.

2 Open the option window of the command for rebuilding surfaces: Choose Edit NURBS > Rebuild Surfaces ☐ (see Figure 11.17).
3 Change the Number of Spans values for U and V. (In our example, you would change U to 8 and keep the value of V at 4.)
4 Complete the command by clicking Rebuild.

The surface is now rebuilt with a simpler and clearer distribution of isoparms. If you're missing any details you had built in before, undo the last step and reconstruct the surface again with slightly higher U and V values.

Rebuild Surface Options

Edit   Help

Rebuild Type ⦿ Uniform ⚬ Reduce
⚬ Match Knots ⚬ No Multiple Knots
⚬ Non-Rational ⚬ End Conditions
⚬ Trim Convert ⚬ Bezier

Parameter Range ⦿ 0 to 1 ⚬ Keep ⚬ 0 to #Spans
Direction ⚬ U ⚬ V ⦿ U and V
Keep ☐ Corners ☐ CVs ☐ NumSpans
Number of Spans U 8
Number of Spans V 4
Degree U ⚬ 1 Linear ⚬ 2 ⦿ 3 Cubic
⚬ 5 ⚬ 7 ⚬ Original
Degree V ⚬ 1 Linear ⚬ 2 ⦿ 3 Cubic
⚬ 5 ⚬ 7 ⚬ Original
☐ Keep Original
Output Geometry ⦿ Nurbs ⚬ Polygons ⚬ Subdiv

Rebuild	Apply	Close

◀ *Figure 11.17 The window for reconstructing surfaces is similar to the window for reconstructing curves. At its default setting the command creates a simpler, more evenly distributed surface.*

The curves are redundant now and you may delete them. If you want to continue working with curves to make changes or add detail, select the four isoparms at the edge of the surface and use the Square or Birail 2 tool to construct a new surface out of these four curves. You can delete the old surface then. Your ultimate goal in this exercise should be to use the fewest and simplest possible curves to create meaningful surfaces.

Before rendering the scene, raise the Tesselation values in the surface's Attribute Editor to achieve a really smooth fender. Check out the shader library for metal shaders or build your own layered shader with a semitransparent varnish layer on top.

◀ *Figure 11.18 A nicely modeled fender waiting for a door, hood, and radiator grille.*

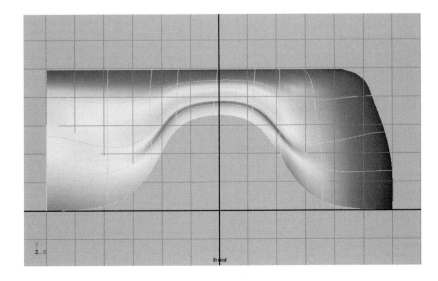

And now for something completely different: Ever tried Find Menu?

MODELING

Nose with a Wart

How do I model a nose with two nostrils, a wart, and freckles?
Theme: Modeling, Rendering
Techniques and tools used: Subdivision Surfaces, Automatic Texture Mapping, 3D Paint Tool

The human nose has one feature that, to the 3D modeler, cries out for Nurbs: its roundness. And it has a feature that is a nightmare to the Nurbs artist: two holes! The polygon specialist, on the other hand, is unfazed by the holes, but is perplexed at having to create a smooth, round surface.

The nose dilemma is easily solved, though, by using subdivision surfaces. Maya offers a whole bunch of prefabricated Subdivision Primitives in its Create menu. We could just as well start with a classic polygon cube. In a surprisingly short time, we'll get a nose that's not only smooth and round, but has two nostrils and even a wart!

In ordinary life, noses very rarely roam around on their own, they're usually an integral part of a whole face. Since the subdivision approach is almost independent from the original topology of a surface you can also use the procedure outlined here for projects where, for example, you start with a sphere for the head. In contrast to the usual modeling process with subdivisions where—as in Chapter 10, with the knobbly man—we mostly use the polygon extrude tool, we'll complete this whole task with only a few local refinements and well-aimed translations and no extrudes at all. At the end, we'll convert the nose to a polygon surface and paint freckles onto it.

1 Begin with a subdivision cube (Create > Subdiv Primitives > Cube) which you scale a little larger (see Figure 12.1).
2 Right-click the cube and use the context menu to make the original Polygon object visible (see Figure 12.2).
3 Use the same context menu to make the vertices of the polygon visible.
4 Select the 12 front vertices and scale them inward (see Figure 12.3).
5 Scale the 6 top vertices inward; move them back. Rescale them again (see Figure 12.4).
6 Translate the lower front vertices (the tip of the nose) to the front (see Figure 12.5).
7 Select the four back faces and delete them (see Figure 12.6).

In these few well-aimed modeling steps, you've created an object that already looks like a nose. Since you didn't extrude anything, you're still working in the one and only subdivision level 0. You can see this in the Channel Box or by using the context menu: Switch to Standard mode and activate

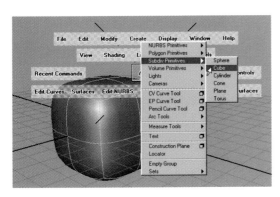

▲ *Figure 12.1 Once there was a primitive subdivision cube.*

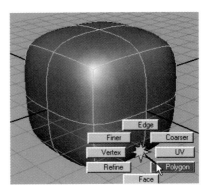

▲ *Figure 12.2 Switch from Standard to Polygon mode.*

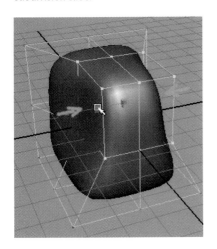

▲ *Figure 12.3 Scaling the polygon vertices gives the cube a basic nose shape—and the subdivision surface follows smoothly.*

Figure 12.5 Giving the nose a
▼ *sharper tip.*

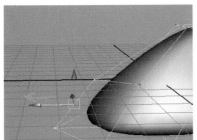

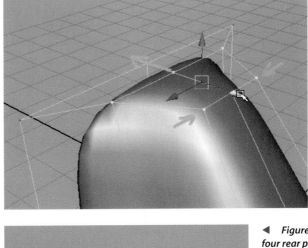

◄ *Figure 12.4 Further scalings and translations shape the base of the nose.*

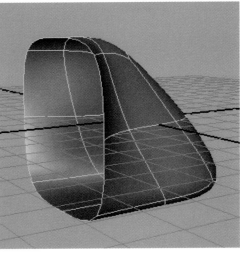

◄ *Figure 12.6 Deleting the four rear polygon faces opens the nose at the back. No Nurbs surface would tolerate such an operation, but the subdivision surface stays totally intact.*

Vertices. The vertices appear as zeros in your modeling window—indicating that you're working in level 0.

If you try to move the lower vertices of the nose upward to shape the nostrils, you'll find that the density of the geometry is not sufficient for doing this. All you can do at this point is pull the whole bottom of the nose upward. But there's an easy way to fix this.

1 If you haven't already done so, switch from the Polygon to the Standard mode.

2 Use the context menu to make the Edges visible.

3 Select the edge that describes the bottom of the nasal septum (the wall between the future nostrils).

4 Use the context menu again and apply the Refine command to the selection (see Figure 12.7).

In addition to level 0, you now have two more levels, 1 and 2, which will allow you to work much more locally. For most character animations (and for this tutorial as well) level 2 is sufficient for modeling the nostrils. You can switch from one level to another either by changing the Display Level setting in the Channel Box or by using the commands Coarser and Finer in the context menu. They let you step up and down in the hierarchy.

1 Make the vertices of level 2 visible. Pick the two rows of four or five vertices each that run parallel to the nasal septum (see Figure 12.8).

2 Choose Modify > Transformation Tools > Proportional Modification Tool and translate the selected vertices upward into the inside of the nose (see Figure 12.9).

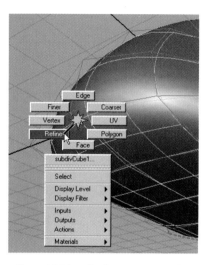

Figure 12.7 Local refinements around ▲
the bottom middle edge of the nose
prepare for two holes.

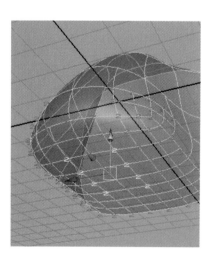

Figure 12.8 Eight vertices in level 2 ▲
prepare us for shaping the nostrils.

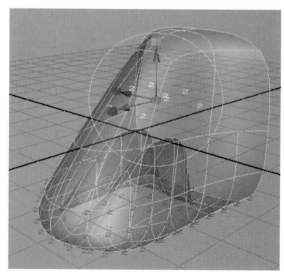

◄ *Figure 12.9 The Proportional Modification Tool translates the eight vertices proportionally up into the nose and forms two nice holes.*

3 Still using the same tool, rescale the vertices so that the middle ones sit higher than their neighbors. Scale and translate the vertices slightly back.

Proportional modification is the tool of choice here because the ordinary translation tool would move all selected vertices up by the same amount. We would have to take a second step and reposition them so that the middle vertices sit higher than the others.

4 Switch to level 1 and, still using the same tool, scale two vertices outward to indicate the outside of the nostrils (see Figure 12.10).

With just these few operations you created the nostrils. Depending on how much detail your project demands, you can leave it like this or spend many more hours working within these three levels. For example, you could try to reproduce a very specific nose, from a real person or from a drawing. Or if you're working on an anatomically correct animation, you may want to move your camera inside the nose, in which case

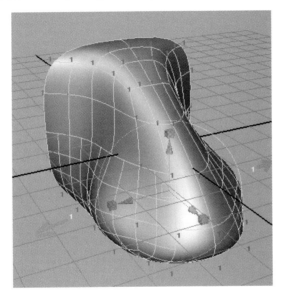

you'd want to detail the nostrils further into the sinus cavity. We won't be going quite that far in the modeling process. Our nose will be done once we add an anatomically imperfect, but still lovely, little wart on the top.

1 Choose a spot on the nose where you'll plant the wart. Switch to, say, level 1, and select just a single vertex in that area.
2 Refine the area around that vertex (see Figure 12.11).
3 Double-click the icon of the translation tool and change its Move Settings from World to Normal.

If you simply move the middle vertex of the refined area outward you'll see that the deformation looks more like a bulge than like a tiny wart (see Figure 12.12). Undo the transformation.

4 Select the middle vertex of the refined area and refine around that area one more time. In the new level, select the middle vertex and move it outwards.

◄ *Figure 12.10 Bulging the nostrils out in level 1.*

Figure 12.11 Local refinements around a level 1 vertex. This is where we'll put ▼ *the wart.*

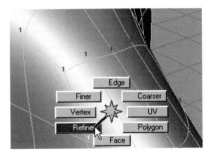

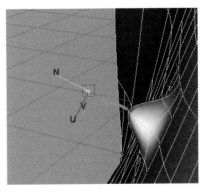

▲ *Figure 12.12 Translation along the surface. The density of geometry—although already refined to level 2—is not sufficient for a little wart.*

Figure 12.13 Refinement for the nose ▶
in level 4. Now very small areas can be
pulled out of the large surface.

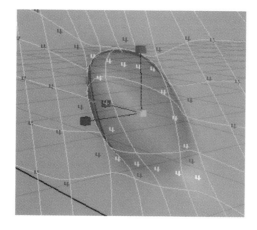

Presumably, you'll need even one more step of refinement (see Figure 12.13). You may want to slightly move outward the vertices around the one you've just pulled out, and scale them inward to tighten the base of the wart (see Figure 12.14). This makes the wart stand out like a cherry.

Now that we're happy with the shape, let's work on the color. In order to paint freckles, convert the modeled nose into a polygon object and tidy up its UV coordinates. This step is important because all the transformations will have warped the UV map of the surface. It's a good idea to save the subdivision scene under a different name at this point—in case you want to return to it later. There's no other way to get back from the polygon nose to a subdivision nose as elegant as the one you've been working on up till now.

1   Select the nose. Choose Modify > Convert > Subdiv to Polygons to open the option window. ◼
2   Raise the value of Subdivisions Per Face from 1 to 2 in order to generate double the amount of polygons.
3   Complete the command by clicking Convert.
4   Choose Edit Polygons > Texture > Automatic Mapping to tidy up the UV mapping of the polygon nose.

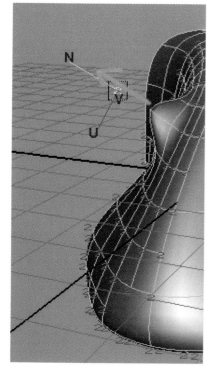

Figure 12.14 The vertices at the base ▲
of the wart are being scaled inward.

Figure 12.15 Modeling views of the ▶
completed nose. In the top right is a
rendered view with two lights.

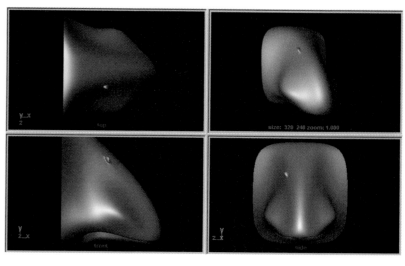

1 Choose F5, Texturing > 3D Paint Tool to open the window for the 3D Paint Tool.

2 Click on Assign Textures and accept the offered settings for the size of the texture.

3 Chose a color (or a brush from the Paint Effects) for the skin. Use a large brush to paint the basic skin color of the nose. Change colors and use a very small brush to paint the freckles. Add a little red to the wart (see Figure 12.16).

Apart from the color channel you can also change other attributes of the 3D Paint Tool. Check out the Attribute to Paint menu. By painting using this technique you create a 2D picture that is mapped onto the nose according to the previously applied UV texture distribution. You can open the picture and repaint it using Photoshop or Paint Effects in its 2D mode, the canvas mode. (See the tutorial in Chapter 28, about texturing a swim ring.)

Using the 3D Paint Tool (with or without Paint Effects brushes) is a rather different way of painting than actually painting within the Paint Effects window (keyboard shortcut 8). Here the strokes you paint are not pixels on a flat texture file, but curves in 3D which render as strokes which either run directly across the surface of the nose or stand out from the surface—like strands of hair growing out of the nostrils. For hair, open the hair section in the Visor.

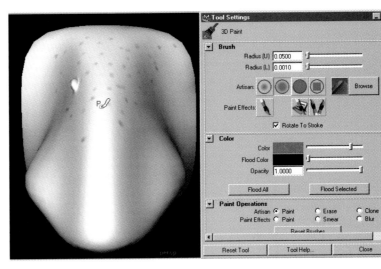

▲ *Figure 12.16 Colorful freckles, painted on with the 3D Paint Tool.*

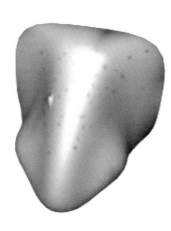

And now for something completely different: Ever set a keyframe for rotation using Shift + E?

FOUR SUITCASES

...But which is the fairest (and the most useful) of them all?
Theme: Modeling
Techniques and tools used: Smooth Polygon, Subdivision Surfaces, Nurbs Primitive, Round Tool

Although modeling the shell of a suitcase sounds simple, it is an excellent example of how different approaches lead to different results. We'll construct four suitcases in four different ways. The last one will be the most attractive, but we won't be able to deform it.

The Polygon Suitcase

The most obvious approach: starting with a polygon cube.

1 Create a polygon cube.
2 Scale its Width to 1.2, its Height to 3, and its Depth to 5.
3 Select the cube and smooth it: Choose F3, Polygons > Smooth.

This operation makes the cube consist of more faces, but not too many (see Figure 13.1).

Handwritten margin notes:

BETTER RESULT IF:
(LIKE P75
ROUNDED SUITCASE)

① USE: POLYGON CUBE

② SIZE IT
③ SELECT ALL OR (BY EDGES)
④ EDIT POLYGON >
BEVEL ▢
OFFSET DISTANCE 0.5
SEGMENTS 3 OR 4

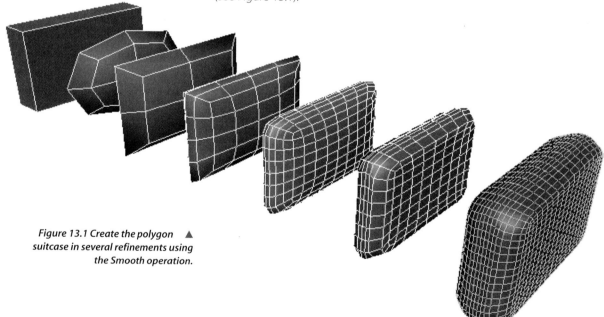

Figure 13.1 Create the polygon ▲
suitcase in several refinements using
the Smooth operation.

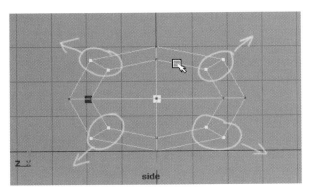

▲ *Figure 13.2 After every Smooth operation, the corner vertices are scaled outward …*

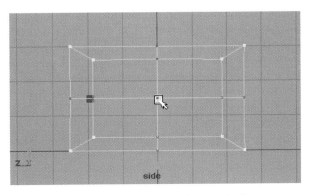

▲ *Figure 13.3 … in order to sharpen the smoothed edges of the suitcase.*

4 In the side view, select all vertices that point to the corners of the cube. Scale them outward (see Figure 13.2). Check the results in the perspective view.

5 Refine the cube by choosing Polygons > Smooth once more, and again scale the diagonal vertices outward in order to get good edges (see Figure 13.3).

6 After a third smooth operation and rescaling look at the sides of the suitcase: Scale them flat.

This completes the modeling of the polygon suitcase.

The Subdivision Suitcase

This process is a little more complicated than the polygon suitcase, but from the very beginning it gives you round edges.

1 Create a subdivision cube: Choose Create > Subdiv Primitives > Cube.

2 Press the 3 key to give a rounded look to the surface.

3 Scale the cube to the proportions of a suitcase.

4 Right-click the suitcase and use the context menu to make the Vertices visible (see Figure 13.4).

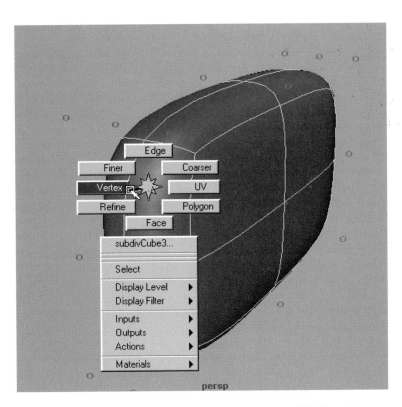

▲ *Figure 13.4 The subdivision suitcase in hierarchy level 0.*

You'll see zeros distributed around the suitcase, indicating vertices in level 0. That's the lowest possible level of refinement, and the only one we have at this point.

5 In the side view, scale the 12 diagonal vertices outward to give the corners and edges their shape (see Figure 13.5).

In level 0, we can't make the corners as sharp as we want to, so we'll have to create a second level.

6 Select the corner vertices you just scaled, and use the context menu's Refine command to refine the area around them (see Figure 13.6).

Now you'll see ones distributed around the corners of the suitcase. If you later decide to continue working in level 0, you can always switch back, using the Coarser command.

7 Rescale the level 1 corner vertices (see Figure 13.7).

Basically, the subdivision suitcase is now complete (see Figure 13.8). If you want to, you can use one of the Crease commands (which we'll discuss further in Chapter 15 about modeling a crooked chair leg). It creates more or less sharp edges and can also be used to model four little knobs on which the suitcase can stand.

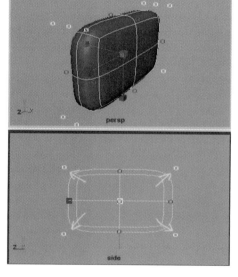

Figure 13.5 Scaling the diagonal ▲
vertices of level 0 outward.

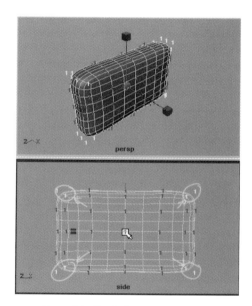

Figure 13.6 The Refine command creates ▲
more detailed geometry at the corners.

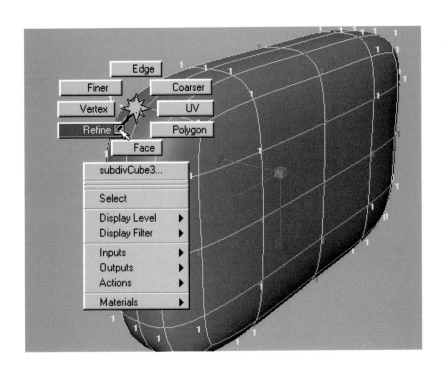

◀ *Figure 13.7 The diagonal vertices of the finer level are scaled outward too.*

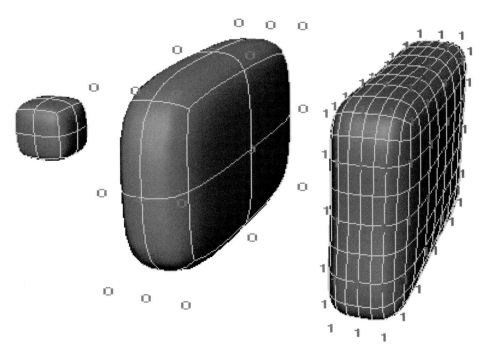

◀ *Figure 13.8 The phases of modeling a suitcase from a subdivision cube.*

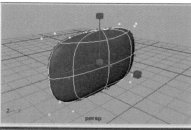

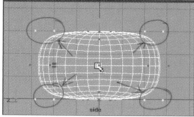

The **Nurbs Sphere** Suitcase

It may seem odd to start with a sphere when we're modeling a rectangular suitcase. But Nurbs spheres are very versatile surfaces indeed.

1 Create a Nurbs sphere. Scale its proportions into the basic shape of a suitcase.
2 Select the corner CVs and scale them outward (see Figure 13.9).
3 Switch to the view from the top, and scale the CVs at the corners close together in one dimension to help shape the edges (see Figure 13.10).
4 Scale the CVs around the two poles of the sphere out horizontally to give the suitcase's top and bottom a flat shape (see Figure 13.11).

This completes our suitcase from a Nurbs sphere—in less time than the others.

◀ *Figure 13.9 A simple Nurbs sphere. It's even rounder than the subdivision suitcase was and requires drastic outward scaling of the corner CVs.*

◀ *Figure 13.10 Scaling the corner CVs together in the top view.*

Figure 13.11 Rescaling the CVs at the top
▼ *and bottom poles.*

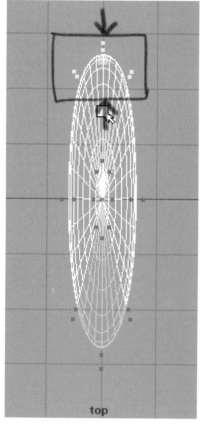

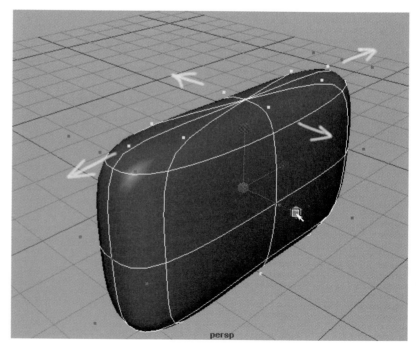

(NURBS CUBE)

The Rounded Suitcase

This final method begins with a Nurbs cube rather than a sphere, and relies heavily on the ~~Round Tool~~ This tool creates a whole bunch of surfaces and yields a really nice-looking suitcase.

1 Create a Nurbs cube.

The Nurbs cube in fact consists of six Nurbs planes, grouped together. The Round Tool that we'll use here requires edges of meeting surfaces, as is the case with these six planes of a Nurbs cube.

But before you apply the command, scale the whole cube into the proportions of a suitcase. To do this, you have to select the group of the cube, not the individual planes. You can either find the group in the Outliner or pick any of the cube's sides and use the Cursor Up key to step up one level in the hierarchy—which is the group.

2 Scale the Nurbs cube to the proportions of a suitcase. For example: Scale X = 1.2, Scale Y = 3, Scale Z = 5.

3 Press the 4 key to see the cube in wireframe mode.

4 Open the option window of the Round tool: Choose F3, Edit NURBS > Round Tool ▢ (see Figure 13.12).

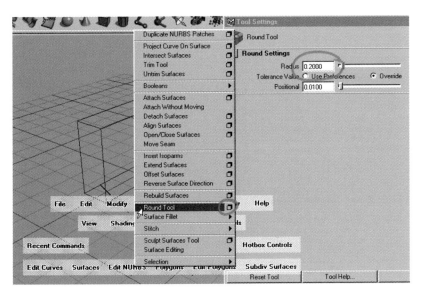

◀ *Figure 13.12 A Nurbs cube ready for the Round operation. A small suitcase needs only a small radius for the rounding.*

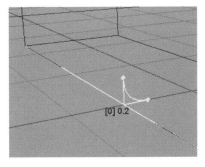

▲ *Figure 13.13 The manipulator offers a radius of 0.2 for the first edge. It can be adjusted interactively.*

5 In the Tool Settings, set the radius to a lower value that fits the size of your cube (see Figure 13.13). If you used the scaling in step 2, a radius of 0.2 will suit it well.

6 Close the option window and follow the instructions in the help line.

*RADIUS
(0.2 number)
can go up/down*

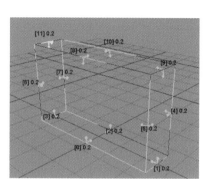

**Figure 13.14 Twelve pairs of edges ▲
are selected. After the Round operation
is completed ...**

**Figure 13.15 ... several new, rounded ▶
surfaces appear. The Channel Box shows
the participating radiuses.**

7 *Select a pair of surface edges that meet*—clicking on any edge of the cube will in fact select two edges that meet there. Select such a pair of edges. You can play with the radius manipulators in the modeling views to adjust the radius.

8 The help line asks you to select further pairs of edges, one after the other. Proceed this way until you have little radius manipulators attached to all 12 pairs of edges (see Figure 13.14).

9 Complete the Round operation by pressing Enter.

The Round Tool makes the cube really round in places where it should be round and leaves it flat where it should remain flat (see Figure 13.15). This is what makes this suitcase look the best. The caps at the corners are especially remarkable—they're independent surfaces and can therefore be textured individually. The round radiuses can be readjusted in the Channel Box: Just open the section *roundConstantRadius1* and enter different values individually or collectively.

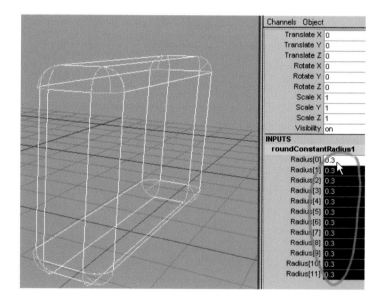

All four approaches to modeling the shell of a suitcase have their own advantages and disadvantages (see Figure 13.16). The last suitcase consists of beautifully shaped individual surfaces, but because they're actually trimmed Nurbs surfaces the whole assemblage can't be deformed properly. The Nurbs sphere suitcase was fast and its geometry is the sparsest of them all, but it has no clear edges. The subdivision suitcase allows local refinement to add details anywhere, but it needs special treatment for texturing. The polygon suitcase had to be rounded several times before it looked somewhat round at all, but it is easy to texture either locally or globally.

SEE NOTE:
P.70
BEST RESULT IF
USE: BEVEL ☐
POLYGON

CON
SUB D
REQUIRES
SPECIAL
TREATMENT
FOR TEXTURING

NURBS SPHERE

(NURB CUBE)
ROUNDED
CON
CAN'T BE
DEFORMED
PROPERLY

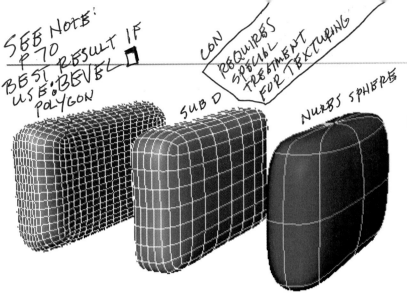
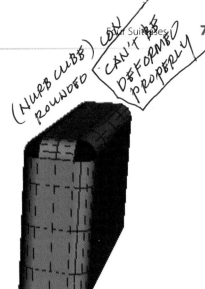

▲ *Figure 13.16 From left to right: polygon, subdivision, Nurbs sphere, and rounded suitcase.*

All of our suitcases are lacking two things: handles for lifting them and a way to open them (see Figure 13.17). If you feel like modeling a handle, start with a halved Nurbs torus or a circle extruded along a path. Opening the suitcases is easy since they all have isoparms or edges running along the opening line where you can detach them. When opening the rounded suitcase you have to put the surfaces from the top and bottom into two separate groups.

◀ *Figure 13.17 Four suitcases, showing four techniques of modeling and four techniques of texturing. The second suitcase from the front (once a Nurbs sphere) was colored using the 3D Paint Tool. The others received procedural textures.*

And now for something completely different: Ever rendered several jobs using RenderPal?

TWO EYES AND A MOUTH

How do I stitch three circular surfaces together to make a face?
Theme: Modeling
Techniques and tools used: Loft, Stitch Tool, Global Stitch

In this tutorial, we'll look at a technique that comes in handy for creating a Nurbs structure with more than two holes—stitching. Why would you want a Nurbs surface with so many holes? Well, say you were modeling a human head. Nurbs modeling provides wonderfully smooth, sweeping surfaces, but it can only produce holes where isoparms (the curves that construct the surface) run together. That means if you start with a Nurbs sphere and open out the two poles to make the mouth and neck, you're stuck—you can't add so much as a single nostril. Of course, you *could* convert your Nurbs head into polygons and keep adding details that way, since polygons allow very local refinement and don't mind if you cut holes. But then you'd lose those elegant soft, radial deformations that Nurbs techniques give you. Likewise, the most modern approach, subdivision surfaces (which you'll notice I use a lot in this book), doesn't provide the radial geometry around the nose and eyes that human anatomy exhibits.

All stitching does is to move the edges of several Nurbs surfaces so close together that they behave like a single surface (without actually being one). We can't apply really heavy deformations to these structures, but in the case of the mouth and eyes, most of the deformation will occur between the structures, so stitching delivers excellent results. Chris Landreth stitched several Nurbs surfaces together to model the face of the first character made with Maya—the Bingo Clown—which became famous in the community.

1 Create a Nurbs circle.
2 Duplicate it once and scale the copy bigger.
3 Shape the inner circle to resemble a mouth (see Figure 14.1).
4 Create a lofted surface from the two curves.
5 Proceed in the same way for each eye.
6 Delete all curves; you don't need them any more (see Figure 14.2).

We're going to stitch the three surfaces together with a single command , Global Stitch. In order to get a feeling for the tool, you might want to try stitching "by hand" using the non-automated variant found at Edit NURBS > Stitch > Stitch Edges Tool (or click the corresponding icon in the toolbar). Follow the illustrations for your pattern.

The Maya help line asks you to select two surface isoparm boundary edges—in this case we'll choose the outer isoparms of the two eye surfaces.

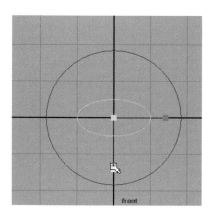

▲ *Figure 14.1 Start with two circles. The inner circle becomes the mouth.*

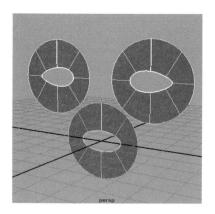

▲ *Figure 14.2 Three Nurbs surfaces— still separate—for the eyes and mouth.*

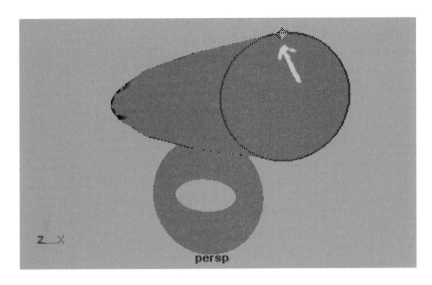

◀   *Figure 14.3 In order to stitch the two eye surfaces together, move the diamond-shaped manipulator toward the center of the face.*

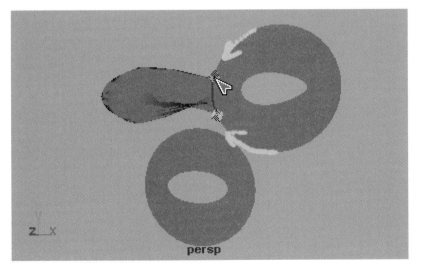

◀   *Figure 14.4 A second manipulator appears (in yellow). Move it to determine which part of the right surface may be touched by the left surface.*

When we apply the command, Maya tries to bring these two circles of isoparms together somehow. Since this is basically impossible (how can the left half of the left eye circle be stitched to the right half of the right eye circle?) the tool appears to fail. But we can restrict the areas where the two circles actually meet by moving the manipulators (they look like little diamonds; see Figure 14.3). This works better, but doesn't satisfy either because we actually need a second pair of manipulators to make the second circle decide which parts of the first one may touch it (see Figure 14.4).

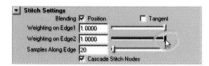

Figure 14.5 The option window of the ▲
Stitch Tool. Two equally important surfaces
need to be equally weighted.

If you've been following along, undo the stitching before we reapply it and open its option window. There we see that one of the edges has the priority over the other. Give both edges the same Weighting (see Figure 14.5), and two pairs of diamonds appear that enable us to restrict both surfaces so they meet only at specific points (see Figure 14.6).

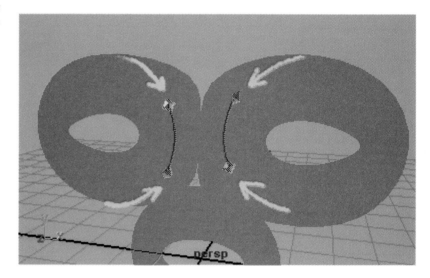

Figure 14.6 Manipulators for the left ▶
surface have appeared. They determine
which part of the left surface may be
touched by the right surface.

After this experiment in manual stitching, undo everything you've tried so far and get ready for the "great stitch."

1 Select all three surfaces. Stitch them all together by choosing F3, Edit NURBS > Stitch > Global Stitch.

You won't see a change unless the surfaces are really close together. Global Stitch in its default setting is shortsighted and looks for surfaces in very close proximity.

2 Open the Attribute Editor of the Global Stitch, which you'll find by opening the Attribute Editor of one of the surfaces and clicking the *globalStitch1* tab at the top (see Figure 14.7).

3 Play with the parameters. The two crucial parameters for Global Stitch are Stitch Partial Edges and Max Separation (the region in which the tool looks for neighboring surface edges).

Since Global Stitch works now, you can begin working on the three surfaces. For example, you may want to move certain hulls of the mouth surface forward and backward to shape the lips (see Figure 14.8). Notice that when you change individual surfaces, the neighboring surfaces try to follow and adjust. But even if you deform all three surfaces with something like the

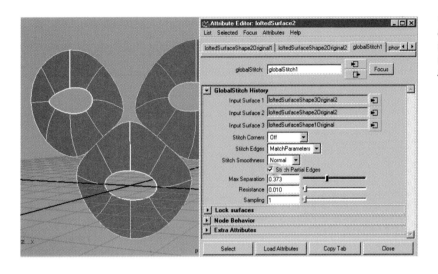

◀   *Figure 14.7 The Global Stitch command stitches several surfaces together automatically. However, the tool needs some fine-tuning in its Attribute Editor.*

Sculpt Deformer the stitches hold fast. If you want to temporarily see the surfaces in their original state, deactivate the Global Stitch by choosing Modify > Enable Nodes > Global Stitch.

Now you can create holes for the ears and the nose without abandoning the comfort of Nurbs modeling. This could be the beginning of modeling a whole head using Stitch tools.

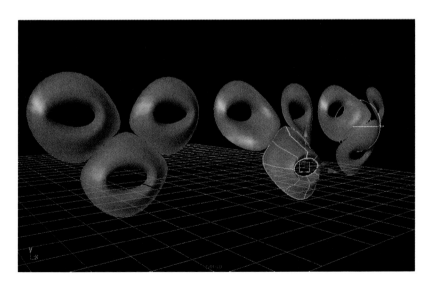

◀   *Figure 14.8 All three surfaces are stitched together (left). In the middle assemblage, the mouth is moved and the eyes follow accordingly. Under the influence of a Sculpt Deformer (right), all three surfaces get warped homogeneously from the center of the face.*

And now for something completely different: Ever duplicated with transform?

CROOKED CHAIR

How do I construct a crooked leg for a crooked chair?
Inspired by Anna Kubik
Theme: Modeling
Techniques and tools used: Subdivision Surfaces, Split
Polygon Tool, Creasing

A chair consists of a couple of cubes scaled long for the backrest and the legs
and another cube scaled flat for the seat. But chairs are only that straight in
the imaginations of mediocre architects and industrial designers. Wood, the
material that most chairs are made of, lives. And so should a wooden chair.

I had the chance to look over the shoulder of Polish animator Anna Kubik
while she was modeling a 3D chair for her thesis animation at a German film
school. She had pencil drawings of a crooked chair with a high backrest lying
next to the keyboard on her desk and, following these drawings, she constructed the chair from the bottom up, over one or two hours. She used only

Figure 15.1 Genesis ▶
of a crooked chair leg.
Right: the modeling view.
Left: the rendered phases
of construction.

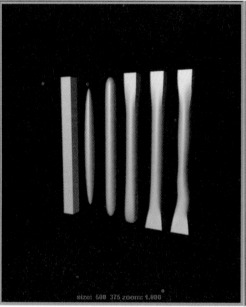

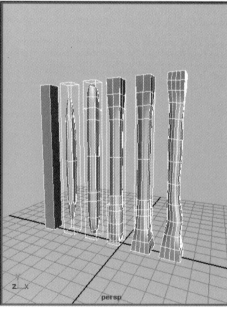

three tools: subdivision surfaces, Split Polygon, and Creasing, which gives round structures sharp edges. If your edition of Maya doesn't have subdivision surfaces, apply the Smooth Polygon command to selected faces. Then all parts of the geometry not selected will remain edgy.

Anna's basic idea was to use the common subdivision modeling technique the other way round. Usually you convert polygon surfaces into subdivs in order to get rounded and smooth edges. She uses subdivs in order to sharpen round-looking regions.

In this tutorial we'll only model a single chair leg, but you may want to continue from there and create a whole chair using the same procedure. And don't laugh at the hours of modeling time Anna spent on her chair. The rendered images of the chair at the end of this chapter speak for themselves. I was impressed with the deliberateness of her work, and it leaves no question in my mind why a chair constructed in minutes by slick duplication and scaling generally looks so cold and boring. Not to mention that in the context of a massive, month-long animation project, a couple of hours is really not much time to spend on modeling a chair that plays a central role in the finished work.

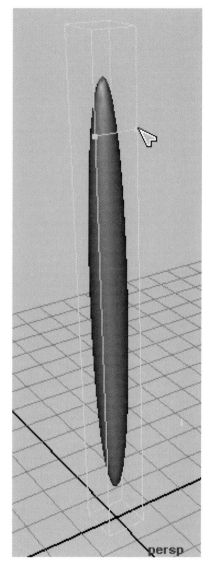

1 Create a polygon cube.

2 Scale it to the length of a chair leg.

3 Convert it into a subdivision surface: Choose Modify > Convert > Polygons to Subdivs.

4 Press the 3 key to see the surface nice and round.

5 Use the context menu to switch to Polygon mode.

6 Choose F3, Edit Polygons > Split Polygon Tool—the tool for splitting polygon faces.

7 Click the upper part of one of the cube's edges to set the first separation point (see Figure 15.2).

8 Click the neighbor edge at about the same height. Before you complete the command with the Enter key, you may want to reposition the split point using the middle mouse button.

9 Repeat the procedure with the other pairs of edges. Let the tool snap to the previously set edge.

10 Split the lower part of the chair leg like you split the upper part.

▲ *Figure 15.2 The Split Polygon Tool divides the front polygon of the chair leg.*

The Split Polygon Tool expects you to click on edges. If you keep the mouse button pressed after the first click, you can move the green dot up and down along the edge. It stops (snaps) when it reaches an existing separation line. You can always release the button and re-edit the point's position using the middle mouse button. After the split, the subdivision surface tries to follow the freshly created polygon faces.

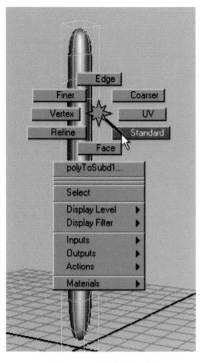

Figure 15.3 Switch back from ▲
Polygon to Standard mode.

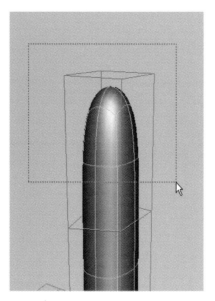

▲ *Figure 15.4 Select eight upper edges for creasing.*

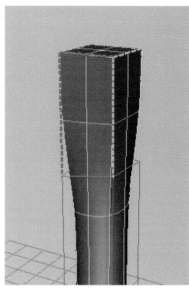

▲ *Figure 15.5 The Full Crease command generates sharp edges.*

1 Switch to Standard mode (see Figure 15.3).
2 Make the Edges visible.
3 Select the eight top edges of the leg (Figure 15.4).
4 Apply the command Subdiv Surfaces > Full Crease Edge/Vertex to the selected edges (see Figure 15.5).
5 Select the eight edges of the lower part of the chair leg.

Figure 15.6 A milder form of crease is ▶
applied to the lower edges.

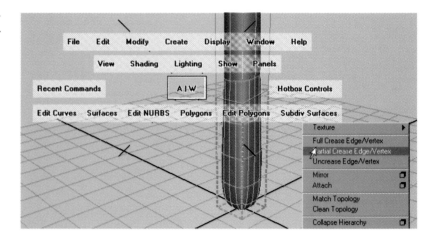

6 Instead of applying the full crease, apply Subdiv Surfaces > Partial Crease Edge/Vertex this time (see Figure 15.6).

Creasing refines the resolution of the surface in the area around the creased edges. You started work with a refinement level of 0; now you also have levels 1 and 2 available for adding more details.

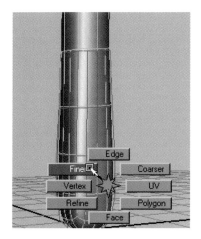

▲   *Figure 15.7 Switching to a higher Polygon to Standard mode.*

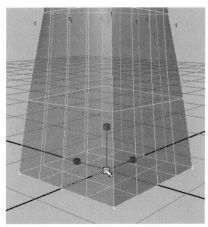

▲   *Figure 15.8 The bottom vertices in level 1 are scaled outward.*

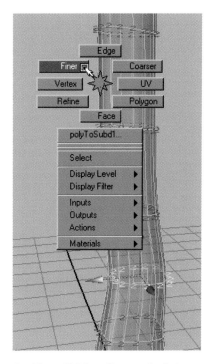

▲   *Figure 15.9 Even finer manipulations and deformations, offered by level 2.*

1 Use the context menu and the command Finer to switch to the next level of hierarchy (see Figure 15.7).

2 In this level, select the lowest edges of the leg and apply one of the two Crease commands to them.

3 Make the Vertices visible.

4 Scale the lowest vertices outward (see Figure 15.8).

5 With the command Finer, switch one level higher.

6 Translate, scale, and rotate vertices in the higher level (see Figure 15.9).

This completes the chair leg. Anna then created a second polygon cube for the next leg and paid as much attention to it as to the first leg. She used some other tricks of subdivision design, too—her own private Maya secrets.

It's up to you whether you want to follow Anna's approach or continue by duplicating and rescaling existing objects. In any case, at the end of the project you will have constructed a chair that you can really relate to, unlike one of those straight chairs that CAD programs spit out.

◀ *Figure 15.10 Work in progress: Several views of Anna Kubik's chair design for her animation "Sally Burton."*

And now for something completely different: Ever clicked on the A|W in the Hotbox and looked to the north?

DYNAMICS

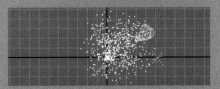

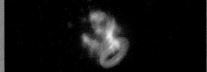

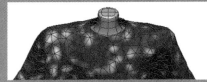

CRASH TEST

How do I simulate a car and driver crashing against a stone wall?
Theme: Dynamics
Techniques and tools used: Active Rigid Body, Passive Rigid Body, Gravity

Real crash tests are expensive because they devour real cars. Simulated crashes are expensive as well, for another reason. Unlike real tests, simulations can be repeated endlessly, but they need extreme computer power. This power is necessary because crash tests have to do with subtle, minuscule adjustments of materials. They not only test the kinds of materials the car is made of, but also how the materials were melted and glued together. Elasticity is a determining factor, but so is the specific point at which each part of the car loses elasticity and breaks. When does it break, how does it break? What happens to the breaking parts, how do they affect the surrounding structures? Do they also break and start a chain reaction?

We cannot answer these questions with Maya. We can replicate the dynamic relationships, but we can't enter the realm of material substances. When we simulate a crash test here, we'll do it only at the lowest level, but it's still impressive enough to make you sympathize with the driver.

1 Create the setup: a street, a wall, a car, and a driver.
2 Position the wall vertically, stretch the street horizontally, place the car slightly above the street, and put the driver inside the car (see Figure 16.1).

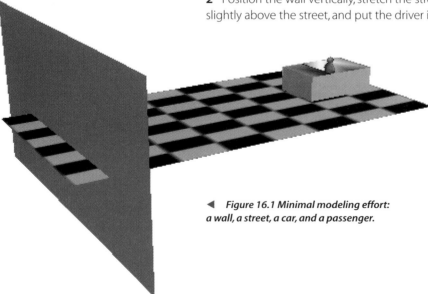

◀ *Figure 16.1 Minimal modeling effort: a wall, a street, a car, and a passenger.*

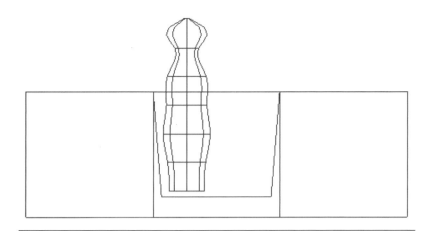

◀ *Figure 16.2 Rigid bodies should not touch each other at the start of the simulation. That's why it's wise to place the driver slightly above the bottom of the car's interior and the car slightly above the street. Shown in wireframe in side view.*

You don't have to model fancy things for a crash test. For the car, a polygon cube with three sections at the top is fine. Scale the car about three grid units long. The car needs some kind of place to put the driver, so extrude the middle face down to create the car's interior. For the driver, you can use a Nurbs cylinder with a little bit of hull scaling (see Figure 16.2).

3   Select the wall and the street and convert both into passive rigid bodies: Choose F4, Soft/Rigid Bodies > Create Passive Rigid Body.

Passive in this context means that these objects will behave as if they have hard shells that can be felt by other objects, but they themselves are not affected by collisions with other objects. This reflects reality—walls and streets don't really care about crazy cars.

4   Select the driver and the car and give both of them the same field of gravity: Choose Fields > Gravity.

When you play back the animation, the car takes its place on the street and the driver stands straight on the bottom of the car's interior. That's all gravity does for us at this point, but it's the starting setup for our simulation.

Make sure that Maya calculates every single frame of the simulation instead of trying to play back the animation in real time while skipping certain frames. Check the option Play every Frame in the Timeline Preferences.

In order to make the simulation a little bit more exciting we'll give the driver and the car a starting speed. In reality, this would be the speed at which the car and driver run against the wall. The speed has to be the same for both the driver and the car, and you can enter this value for both objects together in the Channel Box.

1   Select the driver and the vehicle.

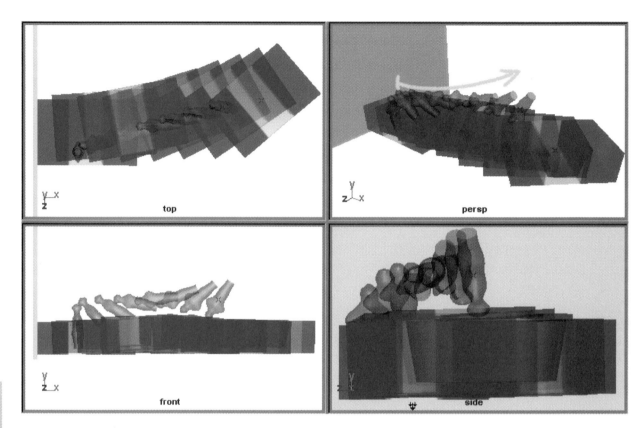

carRigidBody	
Initial Velocity X	-30
Initial Velocity Y	0
Initial Velocity Z	0
Initial Spin X	0
Initial Spin Y	0
Initial Spin Z	0
Center Of Mass X	0
Center Of Mass Y	0
Center Of Mass Z	0
Impulse X	0
Impulse Y	0
Impulse Z	0
Impulse Position X	0
Impulse Position Y	0
Impulse Position Z	0
Spin Impulse X	0
Spin Impulse Y	0
Spin Impulse Z	0
Mass	15
Bounciness	0.6
Damping	0
Static Friction	0.2
Dynamic Friction	0.2
Collision Layer	0

▲   *Figure 16.3 The crash test at 36 km/h (22 mph). Shown here are a couple of frames right after the car touches the wall. It is being hurled to the side. Half a second after the crash, the driver is spinning through the air upside down.*

◄   *Figure 16.4 The most important parameters for the crash: Initial Velocity and Mass.*

2 Depending on the direction your car is facing, in the Channel Box give the parameters Initial Velocity X or Z a positive or negative value of 10.

Say your car is three grid units long, and we'll call it equivalent to a real car that's 3 meters long. Its Initial Velocity of 10 then relates to a speed of 10 meters per second or 36 kilometers per hour (about 22 mph).

When you run the simulation again, both objects lose a little bit of their initial speed due to friction with the ground, but in general they rush at 10 units per second towards the wall and bounce off (see Figure 16.3). In order to see this low-speed crash in real time you'll have to render a Playblast.

3 Select the car and the driver. Raise their Initial Velocity to Autobahn speed: 30 (grid units per second).

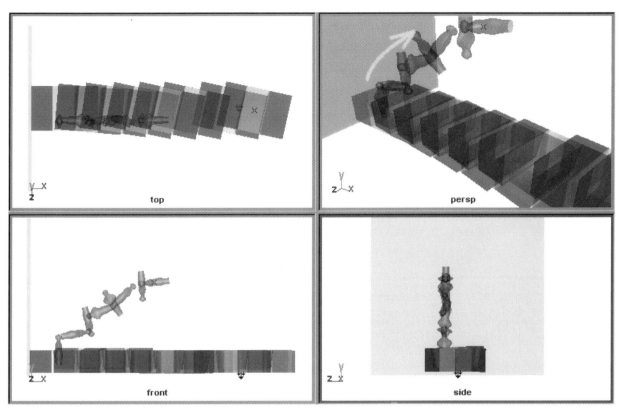

▲   *Figure 16.5 At 66 mph and with more realistic Mass values, the crash is much more drastic. The driver turns over several times in fractions of a second while being hurled out of the car in a wide arc.*

Figure 16.6 A tenth of a second after the crash (rendered with Motion Blur).   ▶

At this speed, the crash occurs much more dramatically. To make our simulation a little more realistic, the next thing we should adjust is the Mass of the participants. Like velocity, mass is an attribute of the Rigid Bodies.

4   Raise the car's Mass from 1 to 15 (see Figure 16.4).

This relates roughly to the weight of a real car in comparison to an average driver's weight. When you see the crash now (see Figures 16.5 and 16.6), you should have no problem imagining what would happen to the driver if the car weren't an open convertible. If you want to continue into that kind of simulation, you should get familiar with Soft Body Dynamics, Springs, and a finely tuned weighting of the Soft Body Goals for the different parts of the body.

And now for something completely different: Ever layered a bumpy transparent Phong over a bright red Blinn?

ERUPTING VOLCANO

How do I make a volcano crater spew fire into the dark night?
Theme: Dynamics, Rendering
Techniques and tools used: Particles, Emit from Surface, Turbulence, Gravity, Fire

Explosions, eruptions, and fire are effects frequently seen in live-action movies. These effects are usually generated with pyrotechnics and later composited into the action scene. But we can simulate many such special effects in Maya—from fireworks to hurricanes—using particles. Particles follow dynamic rules and in order to look convincing they require a lot of expertise from the animator both in their physical behavior and in their texturing.

In this tutorial we'll touch on the essentials of particle animation: creating an emitter, animating its emission rate, and influencing the particles' behavior with turbulence and gravity. Texturing particles is itself a science that goes far beyond the scope of the few pages of this tutorial. But we can get excellent results by simply applying Maya's built in Fire effect to our particles.

1 Create the cone of a volcano either by translating down the upper hulls of a Nurbs cone or by using the Revolve command on a profile curve (see Figure 17.1).
2 Give the volcano a Ramp texture that runs from green (the surrounding landscape) and brown (the outside of the volcano) to red (the crater inside the volcano), as in Figure 17.2.
3 Choose F3, Surfaces > Planar to create a planar surface from one of the circular isoparms inside the crater.

This little interior surface will become our emitter. It can't be constructed at all if the isoparms it's created from aren't planar themselves. Due to construction history, the planar surface updates when you change the shape of the volcano. You don't need to see the plane, so you may as well hide it (CTRL-H).

Figure 17.1 One way of shaping a ▶
volcano cone is with a profile curve and
the Revolve command.

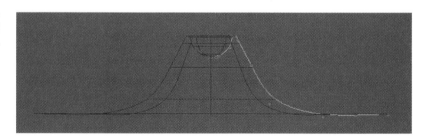

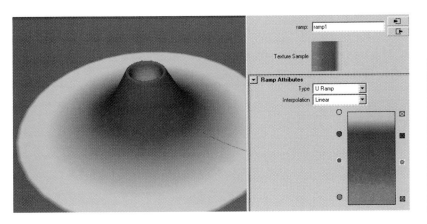

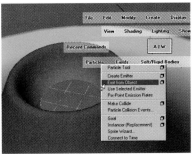

◀ *Figure 17.2 A ramp texture gives the volcano some color.*

▲ *Figure 17.3 The planar surface becomes an emitter of particles.*

1 Switch to Dynamics: F4.

2 With the planar surface selected, choose Particles > Emit from Object (see Figure 17.3).

This makes the surface emit particles, as you can see when you run the simulation. The particles look gray and leave the emitter in all directions. We want them to disperse upward only.

3 In the Channel Box, look up the Emitter Type of *emitter1* (see Figure 17.4). Set it from Omni (all directions) to Surface (along the surface normals).

Play back the animation and you'll see the particles move upward in the direction of the surface normals. If your particles fall down, you can reverse the surface normals by choosing F3, Edit NURBS > Reverse Surface Direction. (This step is necessary if, for example, you have a large sphere that should emit particles inward; the surface normals of a standard sphere point away from its center.)

Right now, our gray particles are equally distributed. They need a force field that will mix them up, so we'll subject them to turbulence.

1 Run the animation for a few frames until you see particles. Select them. Create a turbulence field for them: Choose Fields > Turbulence.

2 The field is selected. Translate its center up, over the top of the volcano (see Figure 17.5). The particle stream should feel the turbulence after it has had a few frames to develop.

3 In the Channel Box, adjust the strength of the field. Try a Magnitude of 1 or even smaller. The field should only mix the particles up a little without really disturbing their general direction.

Now our particles are more jumbled, but they're just shooting straight up. So in this step, we'll apply some gravity to the particles. At first the gravity field will pull them down so strongly that they won't have the slightest chance to

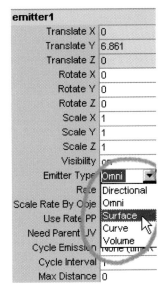

▲ *Figure 17.4 The particles shouldn't leave the emitter going in all directions; we want them to move upward along the surface's normals.*

move upward. The two conflicting forces are the same as for a rocket launch: the strength of gravity versus the speed of emission.

This step also highlights the difference between the emitter and the particles: It's the emitter's job to shoot out particles at a certain speed with a certain density and direction. The emitter doesn't care what happens later, its only concern is to send the particles on their way through the world of forces.

1 Select the particles and give them gravity: Choose Fields > Gravity.
2 Select the emitter (you can best find it in the Outliner; it's parented to the planar surface) and raise its emission Speed.
3 Create a playblast of the animation: Choose Window > Playblast. Unless you have a superfast computer you'll need the playblast to judge the quality of the simulation in real time.
4 Diminish the gravity field and increase the emission speed until the particles shoot a good height above the volcano before gravity grabs them and pulls them down. Try an (emitter1-) Speed of 20 and a (gravity1-) Magnitude of 5 (see Figure 17.6).

Now the particle stream shoots up out of the volcano, is jumbled a little by the turbulence field, and continues moving up until gravity pulls it straight back down. It would be nice to widen the stream of particles so that they don't fall straight back into the crater but land on its sides—like a fountain. The parameter responsible for this spread is the Tangent Speed, which is a feature of the *emitter* rather than the particles.

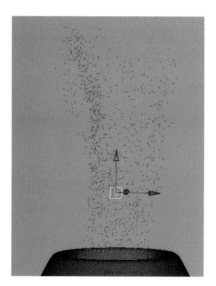

▲ *Figure 17.5 A turbulence field starts mixing the particles up as soon as they leave the crater.*

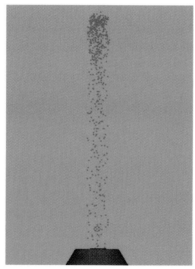

▲ *Figure 17.6 Because of gravity the particles don't vanish into eternity but return to earth after a while.*

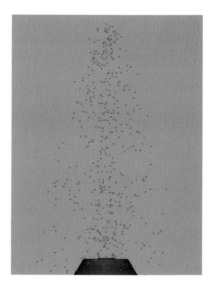

▲ *Figure 17.7 Slightly increasing the Tangent Speed of the emitter widens the stream of particles.*

5 Select the emitter. Set its Tangent Speed from 0 to a small value of, for example, 0.1 (see Figure 17.7).

With the particle stream widened, plenty of particles fall on and through the side of the volcano. If you wanted to make them collide with the terrain and die on collision as if they were extinguished, you'd have to connect them with the surface by choosing Particles > Make Collide. Here's an elegant and natural-looking way to not allow too many particles to reach and fall through the ground. Right now the particles live forever. But we can shorten their lifespan.

1 Open the Attribute Editor of *particle1*. Under the section Lifespan Attributes, change the Lifespan Mode from Live Forever to Random range. This activates the input fields (see Figure 17.8).
2 Enter a value of 4 for Lifespan and set Lifespan Random (the standard deviation from Lifespan) to 0.5.

With this setting, the particles will have a randomly chosen lifespan of between 3.5 and 4.5 seconds before they disappear.

In nature, eruptions don't happen uniformly. They start at zero with nothing happening, then shoot very high for a few moments until they find an equilibrium on a lower level. The key parameter for achieving this is the Rate of the eruption, an attribute of the emitter.

1 Select the emitter. In the Timeline, go to a frame (not too early in the animation) where the eruption should have reached its equilibrium. Right-click the parameter Rate and set a keyframe: Key Selected.
2 Go back to the time where the eruption is just going to start. Raise the emitter Rate to double its value and set another keyframe.
3 Step back another 10 frames (a third of a second). Reduce the Rate to 0 and set a third key (see Figure 17.9).

Now the volcano is still for some time before it erupts mightily, and the eruption then slows to a normal degree. Use the Graph Editor to fine-tune this process.

If you like, you can introduce other forces, such as wind (Air), further turbulences higher up, or a Drag that slows the particles independent of their motion direction. But even without that the particle animation basically suits our needs and we can now move on to making the particles look better.

When you render the scene in the usual way you don't see the particles at all. Only the Hardware Render Buffer (Window > Rendering Editors) would make them visible, during a special rendering process. You would typically

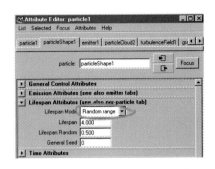

▲ *Figure 17.8 The particles will die after four seconds, give or take half a second.*

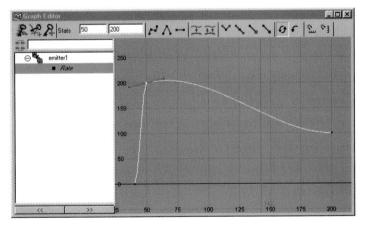

▲ *Figure 17.9 The eruption rate of the volcano is animated. In the Graph Editor you can make changes and fine-tune the animation.*

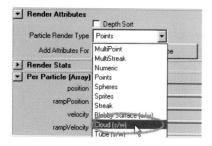

Figure 17.10 Only the two bottom ▲ *choices in the Particle Render Type pull-down menu can be rendered with the usual procedure. The others require the Hardware Render Buffer. Cloud is an appropriate rendering type for a volcano.*

Figure 17.11 particleCloud ▶ *determines the look of the cloud's particles. The middle section of the rendered image on the left shows the particleCloud texture changed from blue to red.*

Figure 17.12 The Create Fire command ▲ *will add fire particles to the much stronger, already existing particles of the volcano eruption.*

see them as dots, strokes, or spheres. After rendering them this way you would have to fit them into the volcano scene with a compositing program like Maya Fusion, Edit, or After Effects. We need a yellow-red fire with subtle transparency effects, so we have to use the normal software rendering process.

Open the particles' Attribute Editor (see Figure 17.10). Under the section Render Attributes, change the Particle Render Type to Cloud (s/w), where *s/w* stands for software (rendering). Cloud basically gives our particles a semitransparent look. When they're rendered you'll see blue clouds. The blue comes from the default shader for particles which you'll find in the Hypershader. It's called *particleCloud1*. If you change the color of *particleCloud1* from blue to red, your volcano will erupt in semitransparent clouds of red (see Figure 17.11).

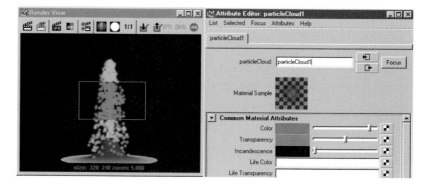

This looks almost nothing like fire, however. If you start playing with the color, maybe mapping it with a ramp, you see that though it was relatively easy to create a somewhat realistic particle animation, it's hard to make it look good. It would take hours to construct *particleCloud1* by hand in the Hypershader so that it not only looked like fire but also behaved like fire when animated. Therefore, for this tutorial we'll take a shortcut and use a prefab fire effect already built into Maya. First we'll create the default fire and then we'll assign its look to the volcano particles. This procedure is not only economical, it also allows you to study the Shader of the fire so you can modify it to your personal needs.

1 Select the planar surface that serves as an emitter.

2 Ignite it: Choose F4, Effects > Create Fire (see Figure 17.12).

When you play back the animation, you see a small fire in the volcano before the eruption you programmed sets in. In the modeling view it looks green, rendered it looks like real flames (see Figure 17.13). In the Hypershader next to *particleCloud1* you'll see the fire's *particleCloud2* shader.

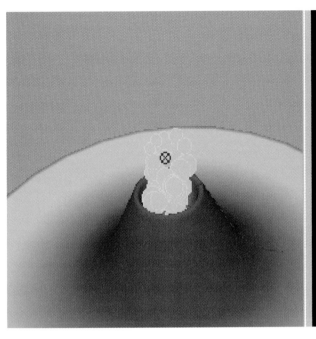
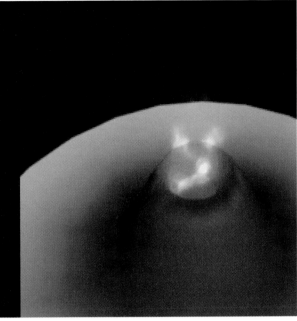

3 Select the particles of the volcano.

4 Open the Hypershader. Find *particleCloud2*, the fire's shader. Right-click and choose Assign Material To Selection to assign it to the particles (see Figure 17.14).

▲ *Figure 17.13 Before the volcano erupts, the fire is already burning in the crater. Left is the perspective view; right, the rendered view.*

◀ *Figure 17.14 The color of the fire is being assigned to the original particles.*

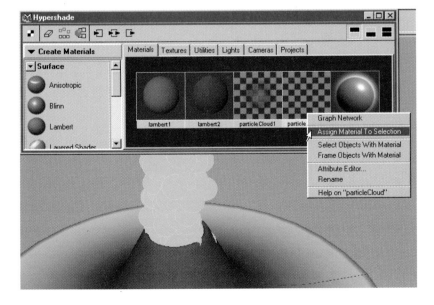

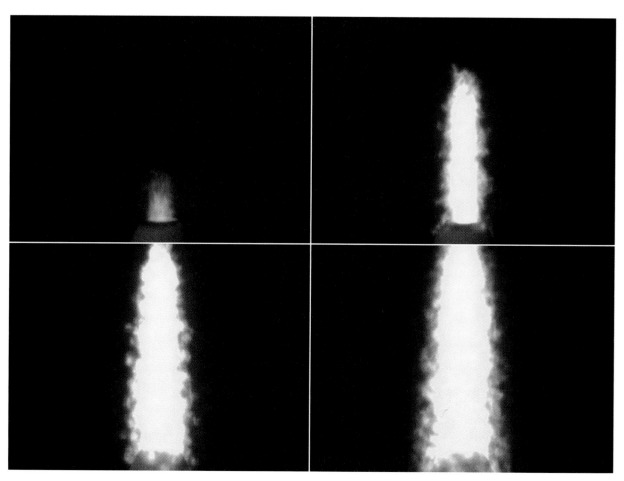

▲ *Figure 17.15 Four rendered phases of the eruption.*

In the modeling views, the particles change their color to green like the fire particles and they follow your animation rather than the original animation parameters of the fire. You can still see the little fire burning inside the crater. You can keep it there or delete *particle2*. It might be a nice touch to keep the little fire so it lingers after the mighty eruption has faded out. The crater then keeps flickering for the rest of the animation.

When you render the scene, the fire looks too thin for a mighty eruption— an indication that the density of particles being emitted is too low. To fix this, in the Channel Box or the Graph Editor raise the emission Rate of *emitter1*. Don't be afraid to use numbers as high as 1,000!

Depending on how big the crater is in your setup, the fire might be too small or too broad. You can select the particles and scale them to an appropriate size.

If it's the *look* of fire that interests you, explore its structure in the Hypershader. The Maya default fire consists of three ramps for color, transparency, and incandescence. In addition to that a 3D-Crater texture serves as a Blob Map. Finally, there are a few expressions at work for other things, such as to determine the Glow. If you are more interested in the *dynamics* of fire, add additional fields and play with the fields, the particle attributes, and the emitter's attributes.

And now for something completely different: Can you build an ear out of three curves?

LET THEM LIE

How do I distribute several objects on a wavy surface in a snap?
Theme: Dynamics
Techniques and tools used: Sculpt Surfaces Tool, Rigid Body Dynamics, Gravity

Very few surfaces are really flat. Even the floor of a new building shows uneven spots, if only at the edges of the carpet. Building such rooms or hilly landscapes in 3D you always run into problems when trying to place objects on top of the ground. You have to invest quite a bit of time in translating and rotating the objects before they actually sit comfortably on the ground instead of hovering above it or penetrating it. With rigid body dynamics this effort vanishes. Not a single repositioning is necessary!

We'll convert the objects we want to sit on the surface into rigid bodies and let them fall under the influence of gravity. This way they'll naturally get placed nicely, just the way we want them to.

1 Create a plane with a dense enough geometry for smooth deformations (see Figure 18.1).
2 Open the option window by choosing Edit NURBS > Sculpt Surfaces Tool ☐ or, if your surface is a polygon plane, choose Edit Polygons > Sculpt Polygons Tool ☐.
3 Use the Artisan brush to deform the surface so it gets real wavy (see Figure 18.2).

1 Create several primitives or import objects from previous projects.

▼ *Figure 18.1 A surface with 20 x 20 patches ...*

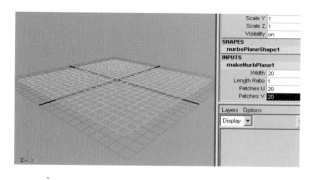

▼ *Figure 18.2 ... is being deformed using an Artisan brush.*

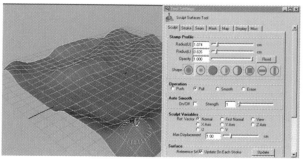

◀ *Figure 18.3 This cube is being placed manually. It's hard to find the point at which it sits comfortably and naturally on the wavy plane. Here it still penetrates the ground in at least two places.*

If you try to place these objects on the surface, you'll see just how hard it is to find that point at which they don't penetrate the ground and don't hover above it either (see Figure 18.3). And even when you find this point, the objects usually don't sit there naturally, they look as if they might slip or they are just plain awkward. In order to fix this you would have to deal with pivots and tiny rotations that would keep you busy for some time.

2 Translate the objects to lie slightly above the ground plane (see Figure 18.4).
3 Convert the plane into a passive rigid body: Choose F4, Soft/Rigid Bodies > Create Passive Rigid Body (see Figure 18.5).

As you may remember from the crash test simulation in Chapter 16, making the ground passive means that it will feel hard to the falling objects but won't move when they hit it.

▲ *Figure 18.4 Starting position for the simulation. Four objects are positioned above the surface, ready to fall.*

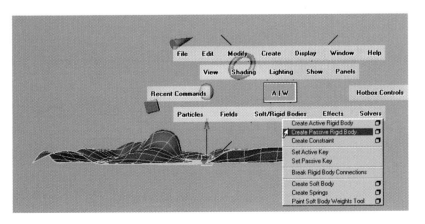

◀ *Figure 18.5 The floor is declared a passive rigid body so it can participate in the simulation.*

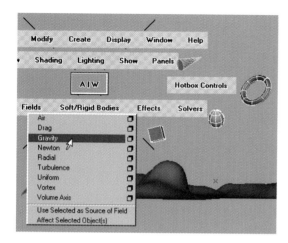

Figure 18.6 Gravity affects the objects. ▲
They become active rigid bodies and are
ready to fall.

4 Select all objects above the ground and give them gravity: Choose Fields > Gravity (see Figure 18.6).

Adding gravity in fact accomplishes two things at the same time: It converts each object into an active rigid body, and it connects them all to a gravity field that will pull them down at 9.8 meters per second squared.

1 Play back the animation (see Figure 18.7).

In order to force Maya to show you the precise simulation frame by frame, open the Preferences and change the Playback Speed from Normal to Play every frame. If some of your objects still penetrate the ground slightly, raise the resolution of the ground plane for the simulation (see Figure 18.8). You'll find the relevant Tesselation Factor in the Attribute Editor of the Rigid Body (not the surface itself) under the Performance Attributes.

If you don't want to let the objects take their time and roll around on the surface before they come to rest, there are several things you can do. Place the objects closer to the ground before they fall; reduce their Bounciness (see Figure 18.9), so they won't jump around much after touching the ground; or raise their Static Friction so they stick to the hills instead of sliding down.

But keep in mind: Whatever you do to the simulation it still remains a simulation. In other words, not everything is predictable.

Figure 18.7 Three phases of the ▶
fall of four objects onto a wavy plane
according to the laws of Sir Isaac New-
ton. The rounder the objects are, the
longer they roll on the surface
until they find peace.

2 If the simulation delivers the setup you want, play it back long enough for the objects to find their final positions and sit still (see Figure 18.10).

3 Stop the simulation and delete the objects' existence as rigid bodies: Choose Edit > Delete All by Type > Rigid Bodies. This command deletes *all* rigid bodies; you don't have to select them.

Figure 18.8 The falling objects are less ▶
likely to penetrate the ground if you raise
the ground plane's Tesselation Factor.

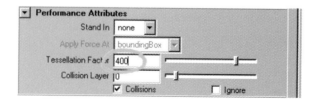

With this approach you can not only place several objects next to each other on a surface, you also can let them fall onto each other so that some of them stack up. Figure 18.11 shows you an arrangement of 2,001 polygon cubes on a flat surface. The simulation used to achieve this arrangement actually consisted of several simulations with only a hundred or so cubes participating in each. A large simulation with all 2,001 polygon cubes participating would have been too much for any PC CPU. Smaller simulations also give you more control over the area where the objects land. Placing the cubes on top of and next to each other by hand would have been a whole day's work.

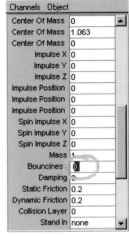

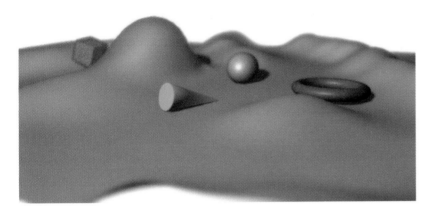

▲ **Figure 18.9 With a Bounciness of 0 the objects lose their elasticity.**

◀ **Figure 18.10 All objects, naturally placed on the surface.**

◀ **Figure 18.11 Chaos of 2,001 cubes after several dynamic simulations (from an animation for German children's television).**

And now for something completely different: Ever made the Outliner disappear and reappear with just two clicks (using the icons at the top right of the screen)?

How do I create a spiral nebula attacking my camera (and finally disappearing into space)?
Theme: Dynamics
Techniques and tools used: Emitter, Expressions, Particle Goal, Goal Weighting, Particle Cloud

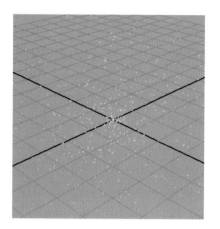

Figure 19.1 Particles emitted from the center in all directions. ▲

Particles follow forces such as gravity and turbulence. That's the main context they're used in. However, they can also follow *goals*—anything from a sphere to a soft body curve or a camera. In this tutorial we'll use Particle Goals to lure a whirling stream of clouds onto our camera. We'll dramatize things by letting the spiral nebula wait a little before it finds our camera, whirls around it, and finally disappears.

1 Create a particle cannon: Choose F5, Particles > Create Emitter (see Figure 19.1).
2 In the Timeline Preferences, set the Playback Speed to Play every Frame.
3 Run the simulation.

Play every Frame is crucial here because we don't want Maya's dynamics module to skip any simulation steps.

Next we'll create a locator that circles around the camera wherever the camera moves. Locators are objects which don't get rendered, as you may remember from Chapter 8.

1 Go to the start of the animation to get a particle-free view of the scene.
2 Create a new camera and a locator.
3 Position the locator above the camera.
4 In Insert mode, move the locator's pivot to the center of the camera, which is the origin of the scene (see Figure 19.2).

With this transformation of the pivot you can get the locator to rotate around the camera. You could use keyframes for that, but a more elegant way is by typing a simple expression.

1 In the Channel Box, click Rotate Z. Use the context menu of the right mouse button to open the Expression Editor.

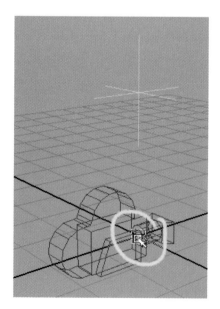

◀ *Figure 19.2 Move the locator's pivot to the center of the camera. You may grid snap it to the center of the scene.*

2 Use the middle mouse button to copy the entry `locator1.rotateZ` from the Selected Obj & Attr field and insert it in the still empty expression field farther down.

3 Complete the expression with `= frame;` (see Figure 19.3).

4 Activate the new expression by clicking Create.

5 Minimize the Expression Editor and play back the animation.

Here's what has happened so far: Particles leave the emitter in all directions and the locator rotates slowly around the camera. Let's make the locator circle much faster.

6 Reopen the Expression Editor and edit the existing expression by multiplying the term `frame` by 10. Click Edit to accept the changes.

The expression `locator1.rotateZ = 10 * frame;` accelerates the rotation by a factor of 10. When you move the camera now, the locator keeps circling around the origin of the scene, not around the center of the camera. We have to parent it to the camera.

7 Select the locator, followed by the camera and press the P key.

This last step makes the locator follow the camera wherever it goes and whichever way it turns. Don't hesitate to move the camera now.

Next, we'll lure the particles in—not to the camera, but to the locator.

1 Select the particles, followed by the locator.

2 Lure the particles to the locator by choosing Particles > Goal (see Figure 19.4).

3 Watch the animation in the perspective view and in the camera view.

Looking through the camera, it seems as if the particle stream attacks and then whirls around us. The perspective window reveals that in fact the particles shoot far beyond the camera. The reason for this overshooting is the weighting of the particles with respect to their goal. Right now that weighting is of medium strength, but we'll fix that.

1 Select the particles (not the emitter), and in the Channel Box locate the attribute Goal Weight[0].

2 Go to frame 100 of the animation.

3 Reduce the value of Goal Weight[0] to 0 (see Figure 19.5).

4 Use the context menu to set a keyframe for this value.

5 Go to frame 300.

6 Raise the value of Goal Weight[0] to 0.2 and set another key.

Now the particles spread in all directions for 100 frames, then are lured toward the locator and whirl around the camera (see Figures 19.6 through 19.10). Looking through the camera things feel much more dramatic now.

1 Animate the motion of the camera between frames 50 and 400.

2 Watch the animation through the camera.

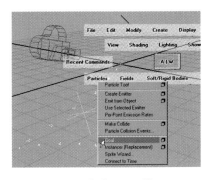

▲ *Figure 19.3 A time-dependant equation will make the locator circle slowly around the origin.*

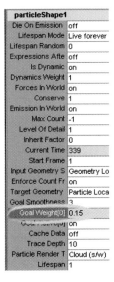

▲ *Figure 19.4 The locator will serve as the particles' goal.*

particleShape1	
Die On Emission	off
Lifespan Mode	Live forever
Lifespan Random	0
Expressions Afte	off
Is Dynamic	on
Dynamics Weight	1
Forces In World	on
Conserve	1
Emission In World	on
Max Count	-1
Level Of Detail	1
Inherit Factor	0
Current Time	339
Start Frame	1
Input Geometry S	Geometry Lo
Enforce Count Fr	on
Target Geometry	Particle Loca
Goal Smoothness	3
Goal Weight[0]	0.15
Goal ...	on
Cache Data	off
Trace Depth	10
Particle Render T	Cloud (s/w)
Lifespan	1

▲ *Figure 19.5 Attributes of the particles in the Channel Box. The Goal Weight determines how attentively the particles follow the target.*

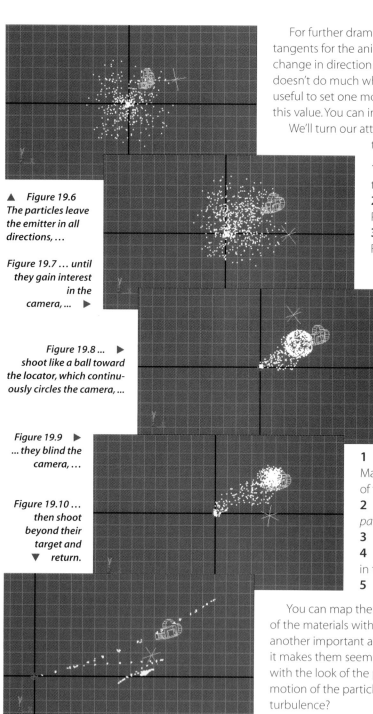

For further dramatization, call up the Graph Editor and set the tangents for the animation of the Goal Weights to flat, so the change in direction starts and ends smoothly. The Goal Weight doesn't do much when set to a value below 0.1, so it might be useful to set one more keyframe leading more quickly from 0 to this value. You can insert keys in the Graph Editor.

We'll turn our attention to the look of the particles now, since they can't be rendered as points.

1 In the Attribute Editor of the particles, open the section Render Attributes.
2 Change the Particle Render Type from Points to Cloud (s/w) (see Figure 19.11).
3 Render the view through the camera (see Figure 19.12).

If all you see is blue when you render the scene, you probably have too many particles that are too big and too close to the camera. You cannot scale particles individually, you have to scale them as a whole. Before actually doing that, though, try increasing the transparency. The particleCloud default shader has a transparency of 0.5. (See Chapter 17 about the erupting volcano for more about particle cloud shading.)

1 Right-click the particles and choose Materials > Material Attributes. This opens the Attribute Editor of the particle shader.
2 In the Attribute Editor, click the *particleCloud1* tab (see Figure 19.13).
3 Change its color and transparency.
4 Create a reference object (for placement only) in the center of the scene.
5 Render the camera view.

You can map the color, the transparency, and other attributes of the materials with textures such as ramps. Incandescence is another important attribute for the shading of particles because it makes them seem to glow by themselves. Once you're satisfied with the look of the particles, you may want to fine-tune the motion of the particle trail. How about a little bit of (animated) turbulence?

▲ *Figure 19.6*
The particles leave the emitter in all directions, …

Figure 19.7 … until they gain interest in the camera, … ▶

Figure 19.8 … ▶
shoot like a ball toward the locator, which continuously circles the camera, …

Figure 19.9 ▶
… they blind the camera, …

Figure 19.10 … then shoot beyond their target and ▼ *return.*

Let's add some suspense. We'll make the particles lose interest in the camera and lure them to another goal.

1 Create a second locator that will serve as the final goal.
2 Move the locator to a point in space that can be seen from the camera at the end of the animation but is far away from it.
3 Select the particles, followed by the new locator, and create a second goal: Choose Particles > Goal.

Two goals for one particle object seems contradictory. But that's exactly what makes goals so flexible. We can set the strength of influence of each goal by changing the goal weight, and thus animate the particles' path simply and effectively.

Right now, the particles don't make it to the camera any more. The crucial parameter which changed this behavior is the weight of the new goal, which you can see in the Channel Box: Goal Weight[1]. This determines how attentively the particles follow the new locator. Since this value is currently set to 0.5, the particles feel its influence and are pulled away from the camera to midway between the first and second locators.

1 Go to frame 400.
2 Select the particles.
3 Set the second locator's Goal Weight[1] to 0 and set a key.
4 Go to frame 500.
5 Set another key for a Goal Weight[1] of 0.5.

Now after 10 seconds the particles lose interest in the camera and focus on the second locator, an invisible target, far, far away. Our flight may continue peacefully.

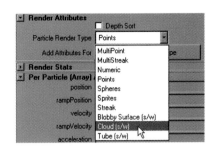

▲ *Figure 19.11 The particles' look is changed from Points to Cloud.*

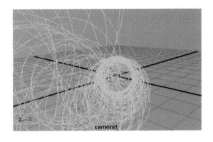

▲ *Figure 19.12 A spiral nebula made of cloudy spheres, as seen through the camera.*

◀ *Figure 19.13 Use the context menu to open the Attribute Editor of the particle-Cloud shader. Change its color from blue to yellow and increase its transparency so the reference object at the center of the scene becomes visible through a thick yellow spiral nebula.*

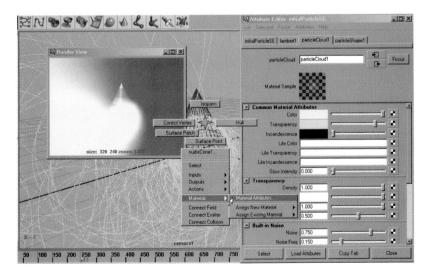

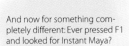

And now for something completely different: Ever pressed F1 and looked for Instant Maya?

PUSHING UP, PULLING DOWN

How do I animate two linked objects—one that wants to move up and another that wants to fall down?
Theme: Dynamics
Techniques and tools used: Dynamic Constraints, Gravity, Fire, Particle Cloud, If...Else Expression

We feel lighter in water, not because there's less gravity but because a competing force pushes us up. This buoyancy really depends on the mass and displaced volume of our body density, but it can be simulated in 3D animation simply using a gravity field working in the opposite direction. By mechanically connecting two objects with conflicting force fields (one pulling up and the other dragging down), we get sophisticated movements whose complexity could never be achieved by ordinary keyframe animation. In this tutorial, we'll set up this situation and enjoy looking at the quarrel for a bit. Then we'll set fire to both objects, make the second object's fire blue, and extinguish the first object's fire whenever it dives below the horizon into the water.

1 Create two objects, such as a torus and a cone.
2 Position them next to each other.
3 Select both objects and open the option window by choosing F4, Soft/Rigid Bodies > Create Constraint ◪ (see Figure 20.1).

Figure 20.1 A constraint will connect the torus and the cone. ▼

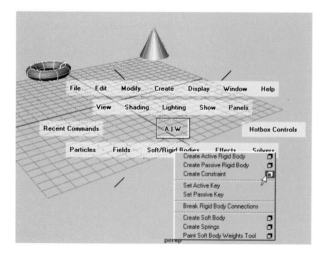

Figure 20.2 Move the Pin Constraint slightly up and to the side before the simulation starts. ▼

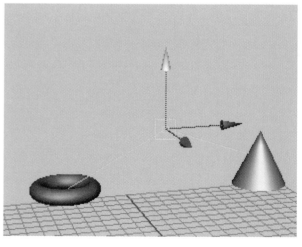

4 In the pull-down menu, select Pin as the Constraint Type and apply the command.

5 Move the pin slightly up and to the side (see Figure 20.2). This will give the motion an extra twist when the simulation starts.

The Nail constraint, by the way, wouldn't be an alternative to the Pin constraint type. Nail works only for one object, like a nail for a picture frame, and we're pinning two objects.

When you run the animation at this point, nothing happens. That's because neither the torus nor the cone is affected by any kind of force.

1 Select the torus and give it gravity: Choose Fields > Gravity.

Playing back the animation shows the torus now whizzing off to the depths, dragging the still forceless cone downwards (see Figure 20.3).

2 Select the cone and apply gravity to it as well.

3 In the Channel Box, reverse the Magnitude of the new gravity field from 9.8 to -9.8 (see Figure 20.4).

With this change the torus still pulls the assemblage down, but the cone tries to move up—which results in very complex motion for the pair (Figure 20.5). If you strengthen either of the gravity fields even a small

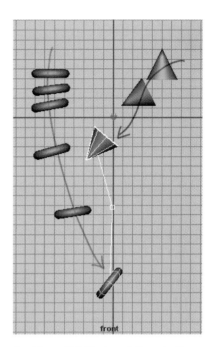

▲ *Figure 20.3 The torus falls under the influence of gravity and pulls the forceless cone down into infinity as well.*

gravityField2

Translate X	0
Translate Y	0
Translate Z	0
Rotate X	0
Rotate Y	0
Rotate Z	0
Scale X	1
Scale Y	1
Scale Z	1
Visibility	on
Magnitude	-9.8
Attenuation	0
Max Distance	-1

▲ *Figure 20.4 A second, reversed gravity field gives the cone a lift.*

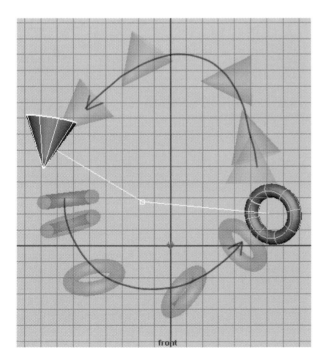

◄ *Figure 20.5 The cone heads up, the torus down. Connected by the Pin Constraint, they have to stay together, however, and thus create a complex yet balanced pattern.*

Figure 20.6 The objects have caught fire, and the flames trail behind them. ▶

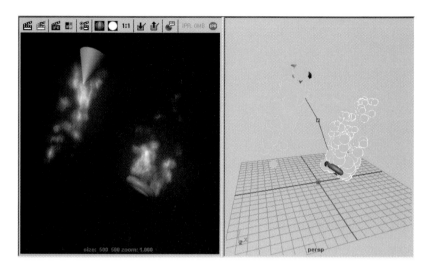

amount, the animation will lose its equilibrium and quickly escape from our view as the stronger of the two forces wins.

1 Select the torus and set fire to it: Choose Effects > Create Fire.

2 Select the cone and set it on fire, too.

3 In the Channel Box, change the cone's Fire Direction Y from 1 to –1.

Figure 20.7 Recoloring the cone's fire ▶
trail from orange to blue.

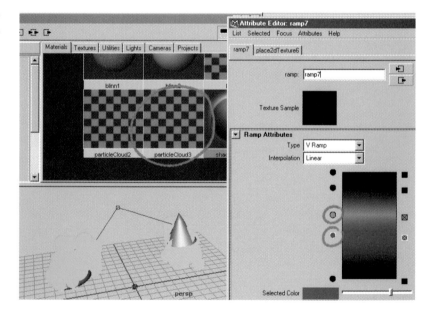

The animation is still the same, but it has a totally different charm (see Figure 20.6). The fires—represented in the modeling views by wildly emitted green spheres—blaze up and down and at the same time follow the lively motion of the cone and torus like the tail of a comet.

4 In the Hypershader, find the material of the cone's fire. Its name is *particleCloud3*.

The number "3" in *particleCloud3*'s name, by the way, comes from the fact that Maya starts any new scene with a default *particleCloud1* shader. So this is actually the second particle cloud we created.

5 In the Attribute Editor of *particleCloud3*, look up Color and Incandescence. Both attributes are mapped to Ramps. Change the red colors of the Ramps to blue (see Figure 20.7).

Now the cone is followed by a smartly color-coordinated trail of blue fire (see Figure 20.8).

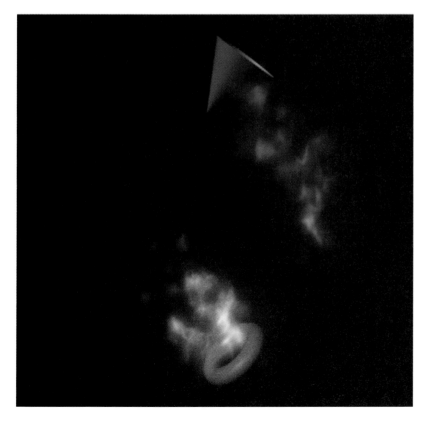

◀ *Figure 20.8 Rendered image at frame 100.*

Figure 20.9 The fire's emission rate is an attribute of the particle emitter. ▼

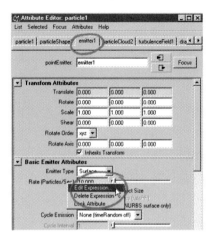

Figure 20.9 The fire's emission rate is an attribute of the particle emitter. ▼

Finally, using only three lines of code, we'll add another accent by putting out the fire on the torus whenever it dives below the horizon line. In order to write the appropriate terms into an equation, you need to know the precise name of the object. You can find this out by clicking on it, and in the Channel Box you'll see the name: *nurbsTorus1*.

1 Select the fire emitted by the torus and open the Attribute Editor (see Figure 20.9). Click the emitter1 tab and find the entry Rate (Particles/Sec).

This attribute determines how many fire particles pour from the cone at a time. It derives its value from a bit of code preinstalled with the default fire effect.

2 Right-click the emission rate to open the Expression Editor.

Here you'll find some lines of code that determine the dynamic output of fire. We'll leave these elaborate lines untouched and just add something at their very beginning. The lines we'll add will change the emission rate to zero whenever the torus dives below the horizon (when its Y translation value becomes less than zero).

To write these new lines, you'll need to know the exact terms for the Y translation value and the emission rate. The Y translation value of *nurbsTorus1* is *nurbsTorus1.translateY*. You'll find the precise term for the emission rate in the first line of the already existing expression; it's *emitter1.rate*.

Figure 20.10 Three new lines of code ▶
in the Expression Editor will put out the torus' fire whenever it dives below the horizon. When it comes up again, the new lines don't apply and the fire will start burning again.

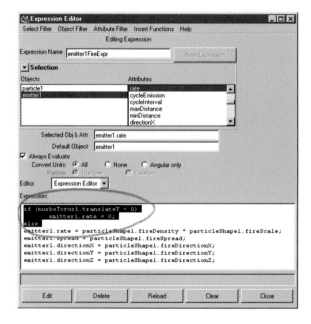

3 Add the following three lines at the beginning of the existing expression (see Figure 20.10). Don't forget the semicolon:

```
if (nurbsTorus1.translateY < 0)
  emitter1.rate = 0 ;
else
```

4 The original expression should continue from here. Apply the changes by clicking the Edit button.

Loosely translated, this code tells Maya "if the Y translation value is less than zero, make the emitter rate zero; otherwise, do what you normally do."

Now when you run the animation, the fire trail separates from the torus as soon as it sinks too low and starts up again when the torus rises above the horizon (see Figure 20.11).

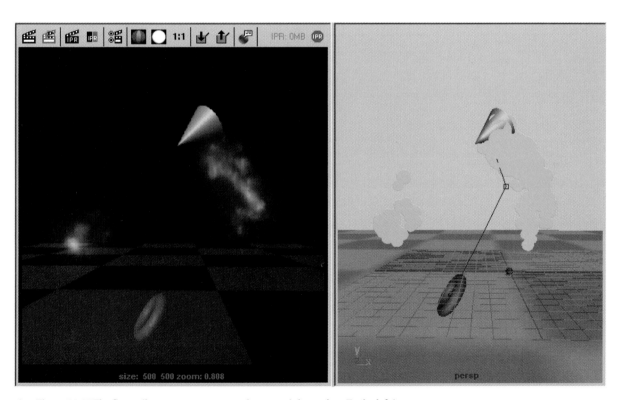

▲ *Figure 20.11 The fire trail separates as soon as the torus sinks too low. To the left is the rendered image with a semitransparent checkerboard serving as the horizon plane.*

And now for something completely different: Ever selected the camera using the View menu?

21

PONCHO

How do I sew a silk poncho and throw it over a torso?
Theme: Cloth, Dynamics
Techniques and tools used: Maya Cloth

Since Maya Cloth saw the light of day, 3D characters haven't had to be modeled to the extreme or covered in insect shells or Lara Croft armor. Now animators have pants, skirts, and shirts at their fingertips. A poncho is just a piece of cloth with one hole where the head fits through—no sleeves, no buttons. This makes it an ideal object to begin our study of the complex world of digital garments.

Cloth holds a unique position in Maya. By sewing pieces of cloth together we're basically modeling a surface; however, Cloth is not located in the modeling menu set F3. The way cloth drapes and fits more or less tightly on a body reminds us of Soft Body Dynamics; however, we won't find it under F4, either. Cloth rules its own roost in the Cloth menu at the top left of the Maya Unlimited window.

Also, Cloth deals with animated characters in an unusual way. The program module that deals with how a garment "feels" itself and the skin of bodies it touches is called the Solver. The Solver needs time to evaluate our setup, relax the garment, and lay it onto the modeled geometry, so we have to wait before we can move our object around. Once the Solver has finished its basic job, however, the simulation runs at a respectable speed and the results are

Figure 21.1 This torso is a rapidly ▶
modeled subdivision surface. You can just as easily start with polygons or Nurbs primitives. The height of the torso (1.5 units here) is important in this tutorial.

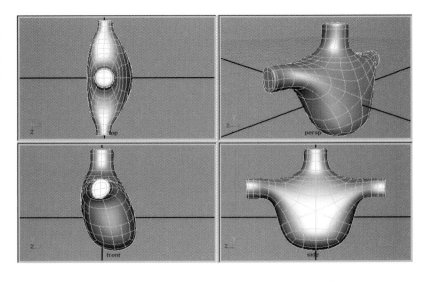

impressive indeed. In particular, Cloth objects don't have that rubbery look so typical of soft bodies. Cloth provides us with mathematical descriptions of the unique properties of different materials like elasticity and shearing. With Cloth we actually see satin, wool, and denim at work.

1 Model a torso or a simplified torso (see Figure 21.1).

The easiest way is to start with a Nurbs sphere and pull out two stumps for the arms and one for the neck. As of Maya 4, Cloth can also handle subdivision surfaces, which is the technique used in the illustrations here. You could also use the polygon approach with a couple of extrudes and the command Polygons > Smooth. (See Chapter 10 for a refresher on this.)

2 Scale the final torso so that it is between 1 and 2 grid units tall and wide.

In Cloth, dimensions matter. Imagine you have a large piece of cloth and sew two pieces of clothing from it: a large dress for an adult woman and a tiny dress for a doll. Although you've used the same material for both, the tiny dress will drape and fit differently onto the doll's surface—it will feel much stiffer than the larger dress on the woman's body. When you model a character like the torso in Maya, the Solver doesn't know how big this character is intended to be. The Solver Scale parameter, which basically coordinates the dimensions of the cloth with the modeled geometry, compensates for this ambiguity.

For modeling the poncho you might want to set the torso to passive by choosing Actions > Template from the context menu. Once you do this, you can still see the torso, but you won't be able to accidentally select it.

1 In the top view, create two concentric Nurbs circles.

2 Move both circles *together* upward so they sit slightly above the shoulders of the torso. You need to move them together because they need to stay in one plane.

3 Scale the outer circle very large. It will eventually be the edge of the cloth covering the whole torso.

4 Scale the inner circle small enough so that it just fits snugly around the neck.

There are two conditions to creating a garment: The first condition requires curves that lie in one plane. The second condition requires curves whose edges form a closed loop.

We still can't create a garment from our two circles because they only satisfy the first condition. But at the moment, our two circles form *two* closed loops which could be used to construct two pieces of cloth, not just one. So we're going to cut the two circles in half and create two new straight curves that connect them along the shoulders. This will give us two closed loops that we can make into two pieces of garment to be stitched together later.

DYNAMICS

1   Use the context menu or press the key F8 to display the Edit Points of both circles.

2   Select all four edit points above the shoulders of the torso (see Figure 21.2).

3   Cut both circles at these points: Choose F3, Edit Curves > Detach Curves (see Figure 21.3).

4   Connect the points of detachment with two new straight curves using the EP Curve Tool and Curve Snapping (key C).

5   Activate the Cloth menu at the top left of the screen.

6   Select both front semicircles and both the new straight curves. (The selection order isn't important.)

7   Create a panel from this closed loop of curves: Choose Cloth > Create Panel (see Figure 21.4).

8   Select both back semicircles plus both the two straight curves and create a second panel from them.

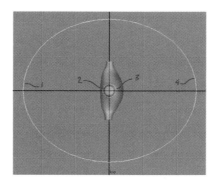

Figure 21.2 Cut the two circles ▲   ▲   *Figure 21.3 This leaves four*
at two points each.   *semicircles—the base geometry*
for the front and back of a poncho.

Figure 21.4 Two connecting straight ▶
curves between the semicircles enable
us to create the panels. The blue arrows
indicate the four curves selected to
create the first panel.

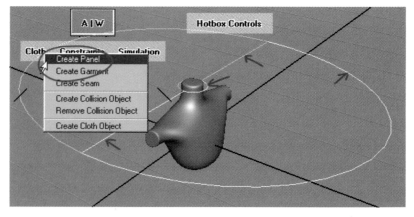

A cloth panel is the preliminary state of a garment and can't be rendered. If you run the cloth simulation right now, the panel just stays put. We need to turn it into a garment, which *can* be rendered and will actually fall onto the torso.

9 Select either of the two panels and create the first garment from it: Choose Cloth > Create Garment.

The garment so far consists of only half a poncho. It will automatically double in size when we stitch the second panel to it.

At this point the garment is built out of only 25 polygons—way too few for a smooth surface. Ultimately, when everything is ready for animation, we'll set the resolution to well over 1,000 polygons in order to get nice pleats and creases, but for our next step an intermediate number of polygons will do.

1 In the Channel Box, raise the Base Resolution of *cpStitcher* from 25 to 300.

Now it's time for stitching. I find stitching a satisfying experience, especially in more complex pieces of clothing. For our poncho, two stitches along the shoulders will do the job. Use the pick mask to deactivate the cloth surfaces now, so you don't accidentally select them.

2 Select the first of the two straight curves above the shoulders.
3 Create a seam from it: Choose Cloth > Create Seam (see Figure 21.5).
4 Select the second curve and create a seam here as well.

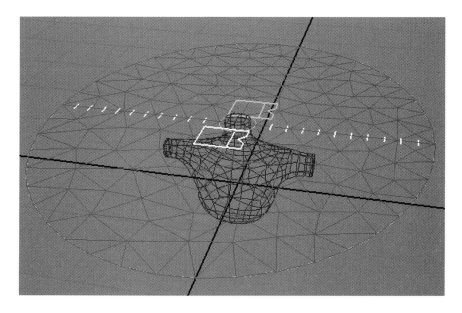

◀ *Figure 21.5 Stitch the front and back together into one garment by creating two seams along the shoulders.*

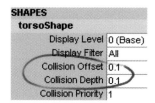

Figure 21.6 The two main factors ▲ ruling the collision of the poncho with the torso are Collision Offset and Depth. The default values of 1 are too high for a torso that's only one or two units big and a poncho that should fit snugly around the neck.

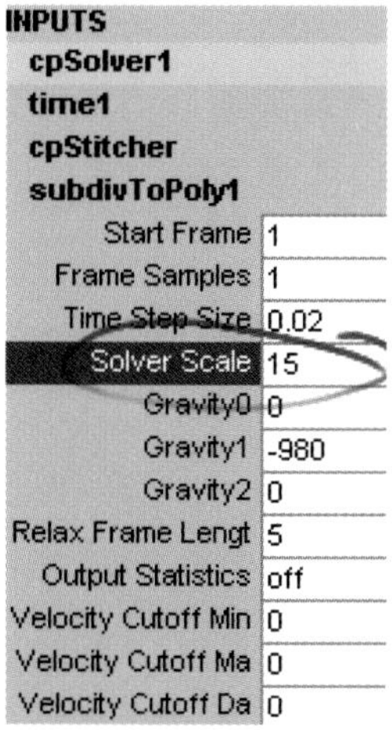

Figure 21.7 With a much higher ▲ Solver Scale, the simulation now behaves like the torso is an adult person, not a doll (Solver Scale 1).

These seams connect the back to the front of the poncho and at the same time create a garment from the back panel. A typical beginner's mistake is to stitch the wrong parts together—for example, if you forget to create the second shoulder seam, the poncho will open there and either hang from the first shoulder or fall to the ground.

So far all you've done is create two panels from six curves, then apply the command Create Garment to one of them, and finally stitch the new garment to the second panel by creating seams. You'd create a more complex piece of clothing in exactly the same way. It's a quick and fun way to get a realistic-looking piece of 3D clothing. Both surfaces don't even need to touch each other before stitching, as was the case with our poncho. If the panels are separate from each other, stitching will connect them by creating new surfaces in between. (The Cloth Tutorial in the *Instant Maya* documentation offers interesting workflows for creating a shirt and pair of jeans.)

When you run the animation now the poncho collapses, falls down, and disappears due to gravity. Leave it down there for a minute and, if you wish, select and hide the original curves and panels. You don't need to see them any more, but you don't want to delete them, either.

1 Select the torso and make it a collision object for the cloth: Choose Cloth > Create Collision Object.

Running the simulation now is likely to disappoint you. The poncho won't relax and drape the torso, but will fly around wildly in gravity until it disappears into infinity. In fact, this is the point at which many Maya Cloth novices throw in the towel. So far everything seemed pretty straightforward, but now it looks like they're getting really complicated. They aren't!

There are two good reasons for the poncho "misbehaving" like this and both can be dealt with easily. The first problem is the way the clothing behaves in combination with geometry and, as I mentioned before, the Solver Scale will fix this. The second has to do with the distance the clothing tries to maintain from the object so that it doesn't penetrate it. This is called the Collision Offset and Depth, and we'll attack it first. The only trick to remember here is that in fact it is not a parameter of the garment but of the collision geometry, that is, the torso.

2 Select the torso and open the Shapes section in the Channel Box. Reduce the values of both Collision Offset and Collision Depth from 1 to 0.1 (see Figure 21.6).

These minor changes have a major effect, and they let the poncho "feel" the torso much more intimately. Before this, the poncho tried to keep a distance of one unit away from the torso and thus flew over and away from it in a big arc.

Now let's have a look at the Solver Scale, so our poncho knows what it's dealing with.

3 Select the poncho. In the Channel Box under Inputs, click the cpSolver1 tab. Raise the Solver Scale to a much higher value than 1, such as 15 (see Figure 21.7).

With a Solver Scale of 1, the poncho behaves like a piece of real cloth in a dollhouse—much too stiff and rough. A Solver Scale of 15, however, tells it we've modeled a life-size poncho and an adult body, so the poncho falls much more smoothly over the geometry (see Figure 21.8). To get an even better simulation, we'll raise the polygonal resolution a second time.

4 Raise the cpStitcher's Base Resolution to 1000.

▲ *Figure 21.8 With the collision parameters decreased and the Solver Scale increased, the poncho falls nicely over the torso. With only 300 polygons per panel some parts of the cloth penetrate the geometry. The color comes from a simple 2D Cloth texture.*

When making changes like this it's wise to delete the simulation cache before running the simulation again: Choose Simulation > Delete Cache. Otherwise, you might see the same cloth behavior as before. The simulation cache is very useful when you're finished with the cloth simulation and start animating the character. It writes simulation data to your hard drive, so Maya doesn't have to do everything over and over again when you rerun the animation.

With the higher resolution, the poncho has a much smoother feel and the simulation takes more time to evaluate (see Figure 21.9). But what kind of material is it? We can pick a fabric in the *cloth properties* section, where we'll find silk, wool, denim, and others. Let's make our poncho a very fine silk.

1 Give the poncho a new fabric: Choose Properties > Create Cloth Properties.
2 Open the Attribute Editor of the new material and open the Material Library there, a small selection of prefabricated materials. In Material Name, select *cpSilk* (see Figure 21.10).
3 Delete the simulation cache (Simulation > Delete Cache) and run the animation anew.

◀ *Figure 21.9 With a resolution of 1000 polygons the poncho drapes perfectly over the torso.*

▲ *Figure 21.10 Cloth properties, from the perspective of physics. Maya provides us with only a few prefab materials. Here, we're clicking on the folder icon to select silk.*

The silk material behaves even more smoothly on the torso, as you'll appreciate when the body moves. In the Attribute Editor you find the physical properties for this behavior, such as Bend Resistance (the lower this value the more pleats you get), Thickness (for a simulated winter coat as opposed to a night-gown), and Friction (between the torso and the poncho as well as between the poncho and itself). The Friction value for silk is of course much lower than that of cotton.

When you animate the torso after the poncho has fallen comfortably over it, the poncho follows the motion naturally. As the torso moves, the poncho creates new pleats, swings, stretches, and relaxes in certain parts. When the torso's motion is fast, Air Damping—an attribute of the cloth's property—becomes an important factor. If you want to let the torso animation start at frame 0 or 1 instead of running up frame after frame for the simulation, use the command Simulation > Start / Stop Simulation. Maya then takes its time to dress the torso without advancing the animation frames.

And now for something completely different: Ever mixed a Paint Effects hand with a birch tree?

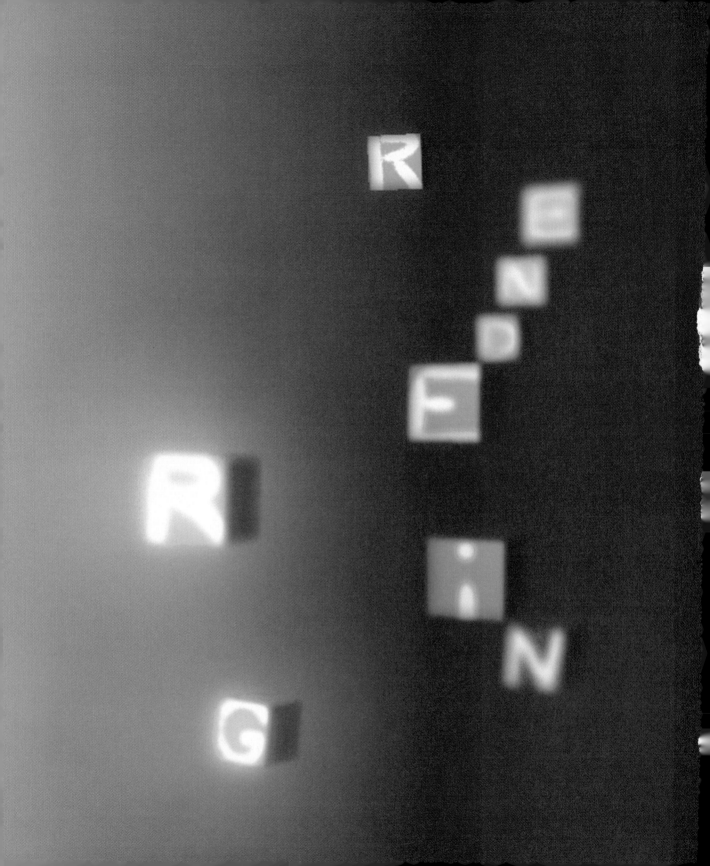

RENDERING

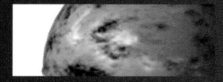

22

MOOD LIGHTING

How do I subtly and randomly move a diffuse light source through a room?
Theme: Rendering, Dynamics
Techniques and tools used: Ambient Light, Nail Constraint, Gravity, Point Constraint

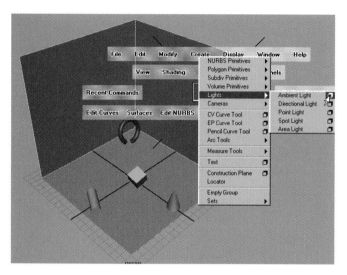

Figure 22.1 Create an ambient light ▲
source to light the scene.

Subtly animated light can considerably enhance a scene in which not much happens otherwise. And it adds a nice extra touch to an already lit and animated scene. The idea in this tutorial is to use real world forces, i.e., Newtonian mechanics, for an ambient light source.

1 Create a room out of a large polygon cylinder, and delete its ceiling and front walls so you have a better view of the room's interior.
2 Distribute a couple of objects in there.
3 Open the option window for the creation of a diffuse light source: Choose Create > Lights > Ambient Light (see Figure 22.1).
4 Make sure that the value for Ambient Shade is greater than 0 (see Figure 22.2).

The smaller the value of Ambient Shade, the more globally the light works. Even though a diffuse light shines everywhere by definition, Maya allows us to raise the intensity of the ambient light locally. We need a light that has a slight local presence, so that it shines brighter in areas where it is itself situated, but still lights all other parts of the scene. With the default value of 0.45, the light is stronger in areas where it actually sits and its influence decreases with distance. A value of 1 for Ambient Shade makes the ambient light behave something like a point light.

5 Create the light.
6 Test-render the scene.

The light appears at the origin of the scene and shines brightest there. You can see this best if you move the light source slightly upward before you render. Unlike all other light sources in Maya, the ambient light reaches surfaces that face away from it, like the darker sides of the cylinder and cone in Figure 22.3.

We'll now create a nail in the (no longer existing) ceiling from which the light can hang and swing. Doing this takes us into the realm of dynamic simulations that Maya houses under the F4 key. Dynamic simulations require

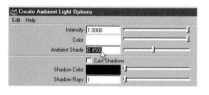

Figure 22.2 With an Ambient Shade value greater than zero, the light has some local presence. ▲

geometry; lights (and other non-geometrical things, such as cameras) can't directly participate in simulations, however. They can only take part indirectly. The trick is to constrain the light to a geometric object like a sphere and actually make the sphere (not the light) hang and swing from the nail in the ceiling.

1 Create a sphere.

2 With the sphere still selected, call up the option window by choosing Soft/Rigid Bodies > Create Constraint ▯ (see Figure 22.4).

3 Make sure that the Constraint Type is set to Nail, and apply the command.

Applying this single command actually makes Maya do two things at once: create the nail and convert the sphere to a dynamic rigid body. In order for the light to swing, we need to position the nail above the sphere.

4 Select the nail in the Outliner (it's called *rigidNailConstraint1*) and drag it up toward the ceiling.

5 Also reposition the sphere a little higher (see Figure 22.5).

The whole assembly should look like a long pendulum hanging from the ceiling (it should be long enough to swing through most of the room). If you play back the simulation, though, nothing happens: The sphere hangs peacefully down from the nail, because it isn't subject to any force.

▲ *Figure 22.3 The ambient light affects the center of the scene more than the surrounding parts, but it also lights those parts of the objects that a point light would leave totally black.*

Figure 22.5 The nail and sphere in their
▼ *starting position.*

▼ *Figure 22.4 It's actually the sphere that will hang from the nail.*

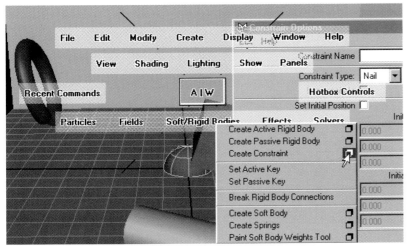

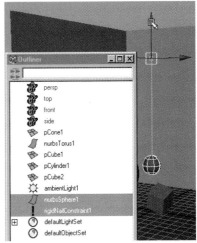

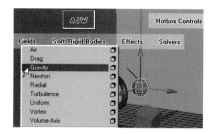

Figure 22.6 The sphere is being ▲
subjected to gravity.

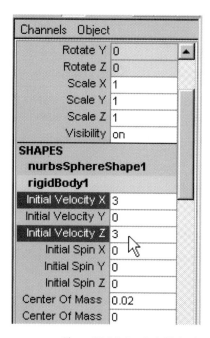

Figure 22.7 Raise the initial ▲
velocities of the sphere.

1 Select the sphere and make it heavy by choosing Fields > Gravity (see Figure 22.6).

2 Pull the sphere sideways, to start the pendulum's oscillation.

3 Play back the animation.

Now the sphere swings back and forth in one plane from the nail. To see the simulation play back precisely, open the Timeline Settings in the preferences and under Real time choose the option Play every frame. This simulation is nice, but it's a little boring; we need to jazz it up a bit.

4 With the sphere selected, in the Channel Box open the section *rigidBody1* and raise the sphere's Initial Velocity in X and Z (see Figure 22.7).

Equipped with these initial horizontal speed components the sphere's motion is no longer restricted to a vertical plane. When you run the simulation now, it swings through a much wider area (see Figure 22.8).

You can tinker with the initial velocities to fit the size of your room, and change other values of *rigidBody1* to add some complexity to the motion.

1 Change the position of the sphere at the beginning of the simulation so that it sweeps through the whole room, but doesn't move outside the room.

When you're satisfied with the motion of the sphere you can constrain the ambient light to it.

2 Press the key F2 to enter the animation section.

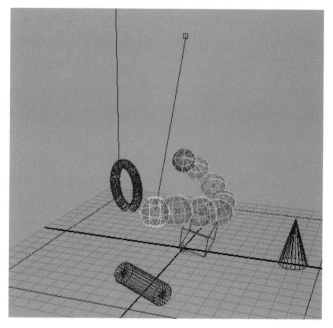

Figure 22.8 The sphere sweeps ▶
through the whole room.

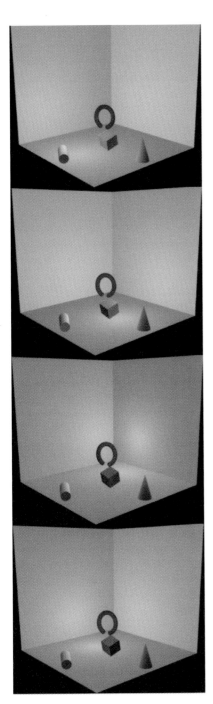

▲ *Figure 22.9 The sphere is hidden. Now the light itself seems to hang from the nail.*

3 Select the sphere, followed by the ambient light, and choose Constrain > Point to constrain the light to the sphere.

You may have noticed that we use two kinds of constrain menus in this tutorial. The command Constrain belongs to the animation section and is used to bind objects to each other, whereas the command Create Constraint in the dynamics menu set only makes sense in connection with dynamic simulations. A nail constraint, for example, is useless without force fields. Instead of using a point constraint, you could also tie the light's motion to the sphere's motion by parenting (choose Edit > Parent). But a point constraint saves us one step by automatically moving the light to the sphere. With parenting you would have to translate the light to the sphere manually.

Now it's time to take one last step, to cover our tracks.

4 Select the sphere and hide it: Ctrl-H (see Figure 22.9).

You now see the ambient light's icon hanging from the nail and sweeping through the room during the simulation. When rendering the animation you see a randomly lit room (see Figure 22.10). When you're basically pleased with the simulation you can bake it to genuine keyframes (choose Edit > Keys > Bake Simulation). Then delete its past as a rigid body (choose Edit > Delete by type > Rigid Bodies) and simplify, scale, and fine-tune its keyframes in the Graph Editor to make the effect of the changeable light more subtle or more drastic.

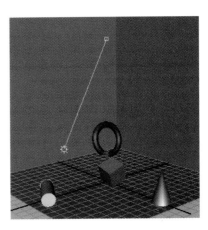

▲ *Figure 22.10 A subtle but impressive effect: The dynamically animated diffuse lighting makes the room more lively.*

And now for something completely different: Ever painted a bald head?

23

ZEBRA CROSSING

How do I create a zebra crossing on a Nurbs plane fading into real-time fog?
Theme: Hardware Rendering
Techniques and tools used: Assign Material per Patch, Hardware Fog

Unlike a polygon, a Nurbs surface doesn't have faces so it only accepts a single texture for the whole surface. If you want to stick a company logo on a Nurbs toaster, for example, you'd normally use the Stencil method. But since the stencil actually floats over the surface (which does have its advantages at times), this method is no help if you want to use the surface parametrization for texture mapping. Say you had a Nurbs street and you wanted to add a center line. You could fiddle with the parameters in the attribute editor of its place2dTexture tab until you got the right look, like in Figure 23.1. But this method isn't exactly interactive, and if you *also* want to add a zebra crossing it fails completely. You'd have to use a layered shader, which is technical overkill for such a simple task. Wouldn't it be nice if we could use the Nurbs surface patches we see in the modeling view to partially and interactively color the street white and gray?

This wish has now come true. Maya 4 allows you to assign individual colors to individual parts of Nurbs surfaces. But there's a major restriction: The results can only be seen using hardware shading—it can't be rendered! Since many artists use Maya in real-time environments, this is still a valuable step forward. But as you work through this tutorial, do keep in mind that you can't use this method (or the new Hardware Fog tool) in a high-end rendered animation. Still, I'm sure you'll appreciate the fast and straightforward way we

Figure 23.1 A tedious method of ▶ assigning street markings to a Nurbs surface using checker textures. Left: the checker texture assigned to the whole surface. Middle: the texture's placement node tuned in order to get zebra markings. Right: the texture tuned in order to get the center line. It's impossible to get both zebra and center-line markings with this procedure.

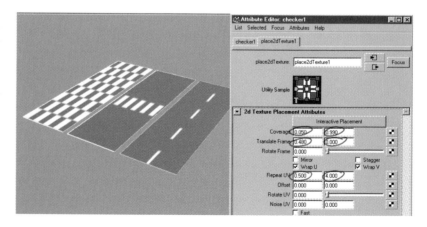

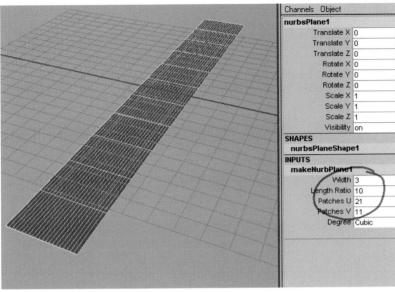

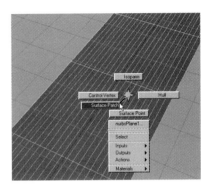

▲ *Figure 23.3 Use the context menu of the surface to make the patches visible and selectable.*

texture a street with a center line and zebra crossing in this tutorial. And about all it requires is good selection skills for the individual patches.

1 Create a Nurbs plane.
2 In the Channel Box, open the section *makeNurbsPlane* and change Width to 3 and Length Ratio to 10.
3 Raise Patches U to 21 and Patches V to 11 (see Figure 23.2).

This makes the plane three units wide and 10 times that length—just like a stretch of road. The number of patches is our template for hardware texturing.

4 Choose Window > Rendering Editors to open the Hypershader. Create a new material for the street's asphalt and another for the white markings.
5 Assign the gray material to the whole street.

This—and only this—is the material the software renderer will use. All color additions we use from here on will only be visible in hardware rendering.

1 Right-click the road to display (only) the Nurbs plane's Surface Patches (see Figure 23.3).

Note: In the selection mask's menu module at the top of the Maya window the Surface Patches are called NURBS Patches (see Figure 23.4). Both terms mean the same thing.

This next step will explore the best way to select individual patches using different modeling views.

2 In the front window, select all the middle patches of the street (see Figure 23.5).

▲ *Figure 23.4 Instead of the context menu, you can use the selection mask at the top of the Maya window to display surface patches.*

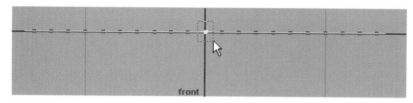

Figure 23.5 In the front view you ▲ can select all the middle patches of the street at once.

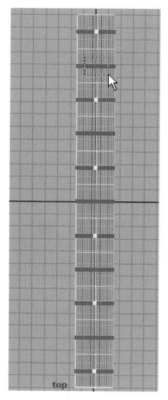

Figure 23.6 In the top view, ▲ remove every second patch from the previous selection.

Figure 23.7 The remaining ▶ patches receive the white material for the street's center line.

3 In the top window, remove every second patch from the selection (Ctrl) (see Figure 23.6).

4 Check the selection in the perspective window. If you accidentally lose the selection, use the Undo command.

5 Open the Hypershader. Right-click the white material and use the command Assign Material To Selection to assign the white marking color to all selected patches (see Figure 23.7).

Once you deselect everything and return from component to object mode, you'll see white stripes along the road (see Figure 23.8). If you had started with a lower resolution of patches in U (along the length of the street), the stripes would be thicker. If for any reason you're unhappy with the size of the markings, choose Edit NURBS > Insert Isoparms to insert new isoparms and thus new patches for the surface.

The density of patches in V (across the width of the street) allows us to create the markings for the zebra crossing.

1 Select pairs of neighboring patches for the zebra crossing. Leave out two patches between each pair of selected patches.

This makes the zebra markings and the space between them twice as thick as the center line markings.

2 Assign the white material to the selected patches (see Figure 23.9).

If a patch that should stay gray accidentally becomes white, just reassign the asphalt gray to it in the same way.

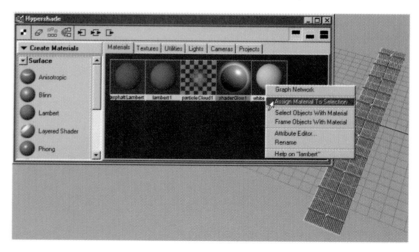

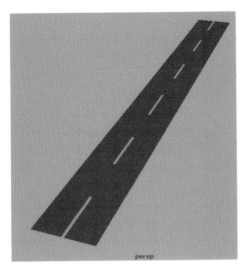

▲   *Figure 23.8 The center line is now visible.*

▲   *Figure 23.9 And now we see the zebra crossing as well.*

▼   *Figure 23.10 The deformed street.*

3   Deform the surface so that the street runs around a bend (see Figure 23.10).

Finally let's use another new effect, only visible in hardware shading and not in rendering: Choose Shading > Hardware Fog (Figure 23.11). You can fine-tune this effect in its option window. It's an excellent presentation tool, especially if you animate the camera and render a playblast. For "real" (meaning software) rendering you need another kind of fog, which the graphics card doesn't deal with: the Environment Fog.

◄   *Figure 23.11 Hardware Fog is ideal for real-time presentations.*

And now for something completely different: Ever compared the dandelion in front of your door with the one in Maya?

WILD THINGS

How do I mix and blend different colors and paint my very own 3D landscape of a meadow with sky and clouds?
Theme: Rendering
Techniques and tools used: Paint Effects, Sky Texture, Depth of Field

When you paint with watercolors or oils you constantly mix colors—otherwise you wouldn't have nearly enough shades for a nice, complex painting. Mixing and blending is crucial. 2D paint programs usually don't give you the option of interactively mixing colors: Instead of mixing blue with yellow, you just pick green. In Maya's Paint Effects, mixing seems to be a well-kept secret, though it's right at the tip of your fingers. Just right-click and you can not only mix colors, but pick brushes and shapes. In this tutorial we'll make extensive use of these mixing techniques and paint a 3D meadow growing wild with several genetically engineered plants and a realistic-looking sky with clouds. Finally, we'll render a gentle little camera motion with depth of field.

Mixing shading and shapes in Maya is so cool that 2D painters would love it. Let's get a feel for the 2D behavior of strokes on a flat plane, simply called "canvas."

1 Press the 8 key to enter the Paint Effects.
2 Choose Paint > Paint Canvas to switch from the 3D to the 2D view.
3 Click on the icon Get Brush and in the Visor open the folder Oil.
4 Select a red brush. Paint a stroke on the empty canvas.

Figure 24.1 The oil color section of ▶
the Paint Effects. We're adding 50 percent
blue to our red brush.

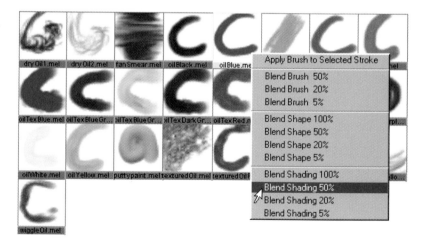

5 *Right*-click (and hold) one of the blue brushes.

6 From the context menu select Blend Shading 50% (see Figure 24.1).

By doing this you dipped your red brush into the blue color and now you have an exact 50 percent mix of the previous red with the new blue color. Like most paint programs, Maya uses the term "brush" for what painters would actually call "color." When we mix colors, we mix the shading and shapes of brushes. Brushes in software mean more than color because they don't just contain color, they also generate different strokes using their unique shapes.

7 Draw a second stroke. It's a mixture of red and blue: purple.

8 In the same way, mix 50 percent of a white brush with the current purple brush and paint a third stroke: It appears as a bright lilac color.

9 Mix 100 percent of a yellow brush to it and paint a fourth stroke: completely yellow.

10 Use 100% Shading of the original red brush to return to where you started (see Figure 24.2).

This way you can mix colors easily and even in fine amounts. The strokes you paint also look different because the oil brushes simulate light as well as color. This makes the strokes look shiny in places and differs from one oil brush to the next. The mix of shading parameters takes this light and reflection information into account.

1 In the Visor, open the folder containing the Feathers (see Figure 24.3). Pick the red feather and paint a feathery stroke.

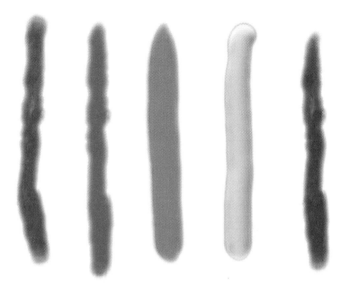

▲ *Figure 24.2 Mixing different oil colors. From left to right: red oil, red oil with 50 percent blue, this mixed with 50 percent white, the result mixed with 100 percent yellow, and finally the yellow brush completely dipped into the original red bucket.*

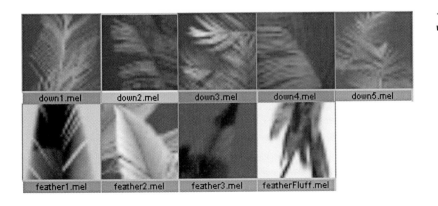

down1.mel	down2.mel	down3.mel	down4.mel	down5.mel
feather1.mel	feather2.mel	feather3.mel	featherFluff.mel	

◀ *Figure 24.3 The library with feathers.*

Figure 24.4 The library with fibers. ▶

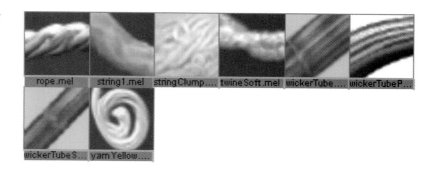

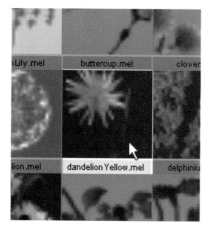

Figure 24.5 The dandelion blossom ▲
in the Flowers section.

2 Open the section Fibers. Right-click the rope named *rope.mel* (see Figure 24.4). Use the command Blend Brush 50% to pick up half of the rope's appearance (which is more than just its color), then paint a second stroke.

That new stroke looks feathery, but it also contains the plaiting information of the rope. Its color is a mix of the feather's red and the rope's beige. Using the command Blend Brush you mix not only shading, but also shape information.

3 Mix 50 percent of the dandelion blossom, *dandelionYellow.mel*, which you'll find under Flowers (see Figure 24.5) with the rope-feather and paint a new stroke.

4 Finish the experiment with 50 percent of the dandelion seed-head.

The dandelion blossom picks up the rope/feather structure and develops only small (50%) blossoms. The dandelion seed-head develops white blossoms and pulls the construction of leaves further away from the feather. The new blossoms only vaguely resemble the structure of the yellow dandelion blossom and seem to approach the size and shape of the seed-head.

Show these and other results to your friends who do 2D computer graphics, and days later when they let you have the computer again, get prepared to grow wild things in 3D (Figure 24.6).

1 Exit the Paint Effects by pressing the 8 key.

2 Create a good-sized Nurbs plane for a landscape.

3 Deform it so it has hills and valleys.

4 Assign a new material to it.

5 Select the landscape and prepare it for the Paint Effects: Choose F5, Paint Effects > Make Paintable.

6 With the 8 key reenter the Paint Effects. If you still see the 2D canvas here, switch to 3D by choosing Paint > Paint Scene.

Now that we have the ground for our meadow, we'll populate it with plants, both organic and genetically engineered.

◀ *Figure 24.6 Mixing colors and shapes. From left to right: red feather, red feather mixed with rope, the result mixed with the dandelion blossom, the result mixed with dandelion seed-head.*

1 In the Visor, select a grass brush from the Grasses folder.

2 Decide where you want your camera to stand and with only a few strokes paint some grass into the landscape there (see Figure 24.7). If the blades of grass seem too small or too big, use the shortcut B (plus the left mouse button) to change their general size.

3 From the folder Flowers, select a flower. Mix it with a tree from the Trees folder and with the new brush paint a new plant into the grass.

4 Leave the Paint Effects.

5 Create and position a new camera. It should sit in the grass and look closely at the flower/trees.

6 Set two kinds of lights: (directional) sunlight and a weaker ambient light.

7 Render the camera view.

8 Change the color of the landscape's floor: Use the pipette of the Color Chooser to adjust the landscape color to the color of the grass.

9 Render again (see Figure 24.8).

Switch back to the Paint Effects again, mix other plants and brushes to your taste, and draw some strokes close to the camera. Keep doing test renderings as you plant the new flowers. If your plants lie outside the camera's view, pick the strokes in the perspective view and reposition them, or just reposition the camera slightly. If you don't like a plant's look, just delete it in the Outliner.

If your computer slows down from all the data in the scene, temporarily hide plants—all the grass, for example. The best tool for switching sets of objects on and off is the Layer Editor.

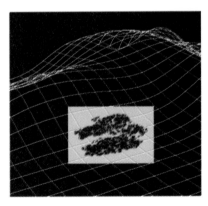

▲ *Figure 24.7 A few strokes of grass on a wide field. The camera will be positioned very close to the grass and see the hill in the background.*

Figure 24.8 First rendering with ▶
ordinary digital grass plus some crossbred
flowers and trees. The blossoms in front
contain a tiny dose of dandelion.

It is easier to create an attractive meadow with the standard Paint Effects plants than with hybrids (see Figure 24.9). For example, if you cross-breed flowers with snails (from the Underwater section) you get surprisingly uninteresting plants with polished stems and blossoms in boring pastel tones. You'll therefore have to weed out lots of your creations.

Figure 24.9 More crossbred plants. ▶
In the middle is a dandelion seed-head
dipped in red oil paint. Very close to the
camera is a semitransparent red leaf that
is actually a blend of a birch tree, grass,
and watercolor.

There are two main things to keep in mind when planting your meadow. First, place the most attractive blossoms very close to the camera and the less attractive plants farther away. Second, don't put too much effort into filling up the landscape! The background can even remain pretty empty since we'll render the scene with a depth of field. That will make objects more blurry the farther they are from the focal plane of the camera.

Our scene is still missing the sky. A black sky is not a pleasant choice for a nature scene. Just a little blue above the horizon has a remarkably positive effect—a ramp texture can enrich the atmosphere of a whole scene. All you need is either a simple background color or an Image Plane mapped to a texture. We'll use the latter approach and map a Sky Texture to the image plane. This method will not only give us nice, natural color settings for the sky at different times of day but also produces clouds and a sun.

1 Open the camera's Attribute Editor. In the Environment section, click Image Plane Create.
2 Under the Placement section, click Fit to Resolution Gate. This ensures that the background texture fills all parts of the rendered image.
3 In the Image Plane Options, select Texture and click on the checker icon next to Texture (see Figure 24.10).
4 In the Create Render Node window, open the Environment Textures section, and choose Env Sky (see Figure 24.11).
5 Render the scene.

Environment Sky offers lots of options for creating a more or less realistic-looking sky. For example, you can change the brightness, create clouds (using a fractal texture), or add atmospheric effects. Since we chose to connect the image plane directly to the camera we can't tilt and pan much because it would expose the fake. If you want to move your camera freely you'll have to map the sky texture to a large sphere that surrounds the whole scene. Since the camera will only move slightly forward into the meadow, the image plane approach is the most straightforward approach for our purposes (see Figure 24.12).

1 In the top window, estimate the distance between the camera and the flowers that are most important to you. If you don't trust your grid unit counting, use the Measure Distance Tool in the Create menu and Point Snapping for placing the tool's locators.
2 Open the camera's Attribute Editor and then the Depth of Field section.
3 Turn on Depth of Field.
4 In the Focus Distance field, enter the distance (estimated or measured) between the camera and the desired focal plane.
5 Render the scene.

▲ *Figure 24.10 The Attribute Editor of the camera's Image Plane: Preparing for a digital sky.*

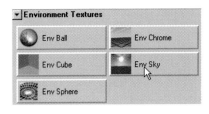

▲ *Figure 24.11 Selecting the texture for the image plane.*

Figure 24.12 A meadow with ▶
clouds and sky.

Figure 24.12 A meadow with ▶
clouds and sky.

If the image shows too much blur, it has too little depth of field (see Figure 24.13), so raise the Focus Region Scale and the F-Stop. The latter value determines how wide the camera lens opens, and a wide-open lens (a low F-Stop value) means less depth of field and more blur. Confusing to computer graphics folks, natural to real-world photographers!

Figure 24.13 Much too little depth of ▶
field, much too much blur: Only the grass
stem at the middle right appears in
(strangely) sharp focus.

◀ *Figure 24.14 Better depth of field: The blur smears the gaps between vegetation areas and puts the red dandelion in pleasingly sharp focus.*

1 When you are happy with the amount of blur, focus exactly on the object which you want to see sharp (see Figure 24.14). The relevant parameter for putting objects in focus is Focus Distance.

2 Go to the end of the animation and set a keyframe for the position of the camera.

3 Go to the beginning of the animation, pull the camera back slightly and set a second key.

4 Render the animation.

Many plants in the Paint Effects carry information about wind, and the wind will blow without our having to do anything to it. Already, when you scrub through the unrendered animation, you can see that many leaves are trembling and the blades of grass and some of your plant creations bend in the wind. Just as it should be in a comfortable landscape for the 3D creatures you have yet to create.

And now for something completely different: Ever let a skeleton walk in Dirk Bialluch's Footsteps?

BLACK HOLE MASK

How do I make an animation of a planet with clouds and a satellite orbit in three separate levels to deliver to the compositing department?
Theme: Rendering
Techniques and tools used: Extrude Surface, Reverse Utility, Black Hole Mask

It's very tempting to do everything within a versatile piece of software like Maya. Once you've constructed and animated a complex scene, rendered hundreds of tests, and even got the light just right, you want to render the whole piece in one go, even if it takes days.

But it's actually better to render in layers and composite it all later. There are two main arguments in favor of this approach. The first is rendering time: You can save rendering time by, for example, rendering all static objects in a layer and compositing the moving objects to it later. For an animation that would normally take ten hours to render, you can sometimes save nine hours. You might argue that rendering time isn't such a big issue any more, especially when dealing with NTSC or PAL (and not cinema) resolution; processing power doesn't cost that much and Maya can distribute rendering jobs on several machines. And if you stick to the Maya renderer, you don't even have to pay for render licenses as is the case with other packages.

The stronger case for rendering in layers is the power of compositing. Compositing can very easily achieve things like changing the color impression of certain parts of the final image, adding a little glow to just one object, or making something look almost cartoonishly flat as it moves across the screen. Also, with compositing software it's very easy to match the color, brightness, and contrast of several layers so that the final image looks more consistent and aesthetically pleasing. It can be very hard for the 3D artist to get colors totally under control since all the materials and lights in the scene have a life of their own, which can drastically affect the final image if the camera moves to another position where, for example, a spotlight causes a glare. If a customer wants the sky to look a little more cheerful and blue, it's no more than a click in a compositing package if the sky was rendered in a separate pass, whereas if you wanted to do it in Maya you'd have to rerender the whole animation.

Figure 25.1 With these settings of the Extrude Tool the small red circle in the middle is extruded along the yellow equator and thus forms a ring. ▼

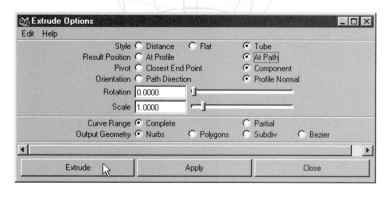

In this tutorial, we'll do nothing fancy—the fancy stuff will have to be done by the compositing artist—but something very pragmatic: We'll prepare three simple layers of a 3D scene for compositing: the sphere of a planet, clouds, and the orbital path of a satellite. We'll also deal with a little modeling, texturing, and transparency.

1 Create a Nurbs sphere and a new material. Use a procedural texture for it like the Crater texture, or use the 3D Paint Tool to paint continents and oceans onto the sphere by hand.

2 Create a small Nurbs circle.

3 Right-click the sphere and use the context menu to display its isoparms. With the little circle still selected, press the Shift key and also select the isoparm along the equator.

4 Open the option window by choosing F3, Surfaces > Extrude.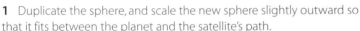

5 Set the Result Position to At Path and the Pivot to Component (see Figure 25.1). These settings ensure that the new surface will be created at the position of the isoparm and not somewhere else.

6 Click Extrude to extrude the small circle along the equator.

7 Scale the new surface—the path of our imaginary satellite—slightly outward so it doesn't penetrate the sphere any more (see Figure 25.2). If you want it to be thinner, scale the little circle, which defines its cross section, smaller.

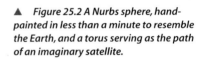

▲ *Figure 25.2 A Nurbs sphere, hand-painted in less than a minute to resemble the Earth, and a torus serving as the path of an imaginary satellite.*

1 Duplicate the sphere, and scale the new sphere slightly outward so that it fits between the planet and the satellite's path.

2 Assign a new Lambert material with a fractal texture to the new sphere—our cloud layer.

3 Render the scene.

In the rendered image the planet is totally covered by the fractal cloud sphere. In order to see the planet again (at least parts of it) we need to give the cloud layer information about transparency, and nothing is more suitable for this than the fractal texture itself.

4 In the Hypershader, open the hierarchy of the cloud material. With the middle mouse button drag the fractal texture onto the Lambert material. In the pop-up menu, chose Transparency as the mapping channel.

When you render the scene the clouds look black and the spaces between

Figure 25.3 The cloud layer ▶
lets parts of the planet show
through. But why are the
clouds black?

them transparent (see Figure 25.3). The problem is that the transparency channel of the cloud sphere interprets the white color of the clouds, instead of the black space between them, as transparent. Therefore, only the black parts of the cloud texture are visible. If we invert the colors of the fractal, we'll run into the same problem in reverse: The parts that are transparent now will become black and opaque. What we need to do is invert only the color values of the fractal that enter the transparency channel of the material (not those that enter the color channel).

1 Break the connection for transparency information between the fractal texture and the Lambert material by selecting and deleting it.

2 Still in the Hypershader, open the Create Utility section and with the middle mouse button drag the Reverse Utility into the work space.

3 Connect the fractal's outColor (see Figure 25.4) to the input channel of the Reverse Utility (see Figure 25.5).

4 Connect the utility's output to the transparency input of the Lambert material (see Figure 25.6).

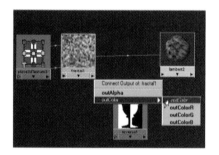

▲   *Figure 25.4 In order to make the clouds transparent at the right place, the color values of the transparency information have to be reversed. The color output of the fractal ...*

▲   *Figure 25.5 ... is being connected to the input of the Reverse Utility. The Reverse Utility inverts the color values ...*

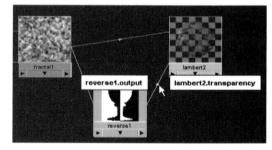

▲   *Figure 25.6 ... and hands them over to the transparency channel of the cloud material.*

Now the white (not the black) parts of the clouds are being interpreted as opaque. When rendering you see white clouds with spaces between them where the planet shows through (see Figure 25.7). If you click on the round white icon in the render window, you'll see the alpha mask of the image. Here the clouds show the correct nice, fluffy edges (see Figure 25.8).

Note that although we've been talking about black and white, Maya actually uses grayscale information for rendering transparency. So the Reverse Utility makes a dark gray turn into a bright gray and leaves middle tones untouched. The fluffy appearance of clouds comes from more and less transparent areas, that is, different levels of gray.

Before we go on to render separate layers of the scene, it's worth the effort to pack the elements of each rendering step into individual layers that can easily be switched on and off. You'll appreciate this when you use one click on the visibility box in the Layer Editor to make the cloud layer temporarily disappear, leaving the planet layer alone in the modeling view. The Layer Editor is located directly beneath the Outliner and is self-explanatory (see Figure 25.9).

Many 3D animators seem to have an aversion to alpha channels and masks. And really, a 3D artist has other things to focus on, and no time to be an "alpha expert." But you do need to know what you're delivering to your colleague or customer. The standard image rendered in Maya contains a mask channel that basically says: Here (where it's white) is an object, here (where it's black) you can look through to infinity. The mask channel will only fill the image completely with white if you have a background filled with images or a large image like a sphere for a sky texture.

If you simply set the planet and clouds in our tutorial invisible in order to render the satellite's path (see Figure 25.10) and give the rendered image to your colleague in the compositing department, you'll get an earful. Your colleague will rightly complain that the ring contains no information about where in the composition it should be visible (in front) and where the planet and the clouds should sit in front and hide it (the back) (see Figure 25.11). The front and back of objects (their displayed and hidden areas) are the most crucial things for a compositing artist to know, and you—the 3D artist—need to deliver that information correctly.

Let's suppose you hide the planet and the satellite layer and render only the cloud layer—your colleague will run into the same problem. Loaded into a compositing program the back of the cloud sphere will shine through as if the sphere were made of glass (see Figure 25.12).

The basic procedure for rendering in layers for compositing goes like this: Start with what's farthest away and render this layer first, without the other layers. Next, display the second layer and set the first layer to black so that it delivers no more color information, but still tells the alpha channel: Here I am! This option—essential for compositing —is called the Black Hole mask and is a feature of the object's material, not of the object

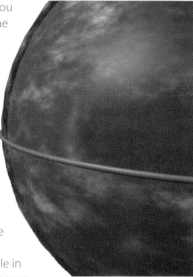

▲ *Figure 25.7 The reversed transparency channel produces the proper cloud effect.*

▲ *Figure 25.8 The cloud layer's transparency mask channel. The edge shows the nice, fluffy appearance of clouds.*

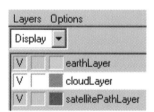

▲ *Figure 25.9 Each level for rendering should be packed into its own layer using the Layer Editor. Here the objects contained in a layer can easily be switched on and off by clicking on the V (visible) box.*

◀ *Figure 25.11 Only the satellite ring's mask channel displayed. Although it looks perfect to the 3D artist, it's useless to a compositing colleague because it lacks information about where the ring and the other layers are supposed to cover each other in the final composition.*

▲ *Figure 25.10 The satellite ring rendered, with invisible planet and cloud layers.*

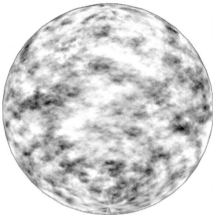

◀ *Figure 25.12 Hidden satellite and planet layers, with only the clouds rendered. You couldn't use this picture for compositing, because the back of the cloud sphere would shine through and lie on top of the planet and the satellite ring.*

itself. Render the second pass with layer 2 visible and layer 1 set to Black Hole mask. When rendering the third layer, set layers 1 and 2 to Black Hole mask and make only layer 3 visible. And so on.

In our example, the appropriate procedure (which will keep the interpersonal relationships in the company intact), goes like this:

1 Switch the satellite path and the clouds to invisible.

2 Render the planet sphere just as it is and keep the rendered image for the compositing colleague (see Figure 25.13).

Figure 25.13 The first correctly ▶
rendered pass: The layer of the planet is rendered normally; both other layers are invisible (left).

Figure 25.14 The planet's ▶
mask (right).

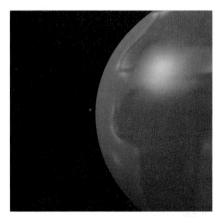

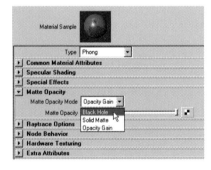

Figure 25.15 Before rendering the ▲
second pass, the planet's mask has to be set to Black Hole.

Figure 25.16 Rendered clouds, with ▶
the planet layer. The effect of the planet's Black Hole mask (left) ...

Figure 25.17 ... is visible in the cloud ▶
layer's alpha channel. Here's a detailed view with the edge of the planet layer visible as completely white. The mask hides all clouds behind the planet (right).

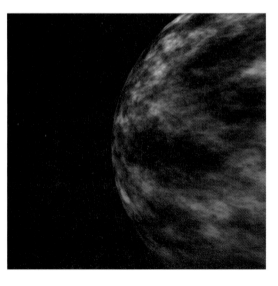

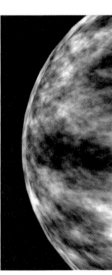

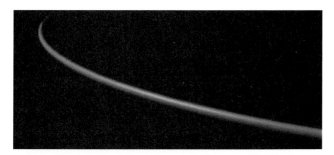

◄ *Figure 25.18 Third correctly rendered pass: the satellite layer. The ring hides the cloud and planet spheres only in front and disappears in the back. The Black Hole masks of the cloud and planet layers participate in this rendering.*

◄ *Figure 25.19 The alpha channel of the satellite path. The ring's mask respects the presence of clouds and planet.*

3 Open the Attribute Editor of the planet's material (not its geometry) and in the section Matte Opacity, set the Mode to Black Hole (see Figure 25.14 and Figure 25.15).

4 Make the cloud layer visible.

5 Render the second pass, the cloud layer (see Figure 25.16). This rendering will take into account the alpha information of where the planet is, but won't render the planet's color (see Figure 25.17). Keep this image for your compositing colleague.

6 Set the mask of the cloud material to Black Hole.

7 Make the satellite layer visible.

8 Render the third pass, the satellite path (see Figure 25.18). Keep this image for your compositing colleague (see Figure 25.19).

Any compositing program will be able to deal correctly with these three images (or, in the case of an animation, with *series* of images). A young Polish animator who won a couple of prizes for his first 3D animation once said to me there's no point in rendering in layers, because he wouldn't give his material out to others anyway. Maybe he had previously had bad experiences. And indeed, compositing is no less difficult an art than 3D animation. More likely however, his problem (and many other animators') is an inability to let go, a lack of confidence in the compositing artist, who, by the way, can learn a lot from the 3D world as well.

Since this is a book on 3D animation, we'll end this tutorial without a fancy composited image of the three layers. Let's leave that to the compositing department.

And now for something completely different: Ever made the Timeline invisible?

THE SHADOW OF THE TREES

How do I add the shadow of a birch tree's leaves and branches, swaying in the wind, to my cheerless 3D-room?
Theme: Rendering, Animation
Techniques and tools used: Paint Effects

A nice, simple technique for making a light source look more interesting is to add a filter to it. In Maya you can do this either by changing the color of the light or by mapping a texture to this color. By animating the texture you can simulate effects like the shadow of moving clouds or venetian blinds being pulled up.

With the advent of the Paint Effects we can use digital trees to spruce up the light and shadow of a scene. Sometimes we don't even have to see the actual trees—just their shadows.

1 Create a polygon cube large enough to move the camera around in comfortably.

2 Extrude one of its side faces, scale the extruded face to the size of a window, and delete it (see Figure 26.1).

3 Create an ambient light and sunlight (a directional light). Position the latter so that it shines through the window into the room and reaches parts of the floor and the back or side walls. Choose Panels > Look Through Selected to place the directional light interactively.

4 In the Attribute Editor of the light, switch on its Depth Map Shadows and set the Dmap Filter Size to a higher value, like 3. This will soften the edges of the shadows.

5 To give the eye something to focus on, add two columns made from cylinders to the room.

6 Create a new camera and position it in the room. If necessary, reduce its focal length to give it a wider view.

7 Render an image of the interior of the room with its two columns and the light shining in through the window (see Figure 26.2).

We've set up our room now, and I think you'll agree that it's dull. There's nothing really wrong with it, exactly; it just reinforces the cliché of computer-generated worlds looking artificial and boring.

Figure 26.1 A polygon cube whose front face was extruded, scaled, and deleted to make a window. ▼

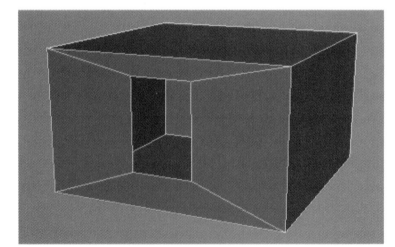

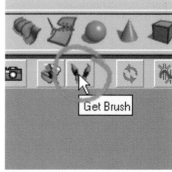

◄ *Figure 26.2 A wide-angle camera sits in the room and looks at the shadows produced by the sunlight.*

▲ *Figure 26.3 Clicking this icon opens the Visor with its wide variety of brushes.*

1 In the perspective window, press the 8 key and switch to the Paint Effects (Figure 26.3).

2 From the Trees section, get the brush called *BirchBlowingLight.mel*—it will allow you to paint a birch tree swaying in the wind (Figure 26.4).

Once you've chosen the brush, move your pointer over the ground plane, without clicking yet, and you can determine the tree's size. The brush is probably much too small compared to the large dimensions of the room. In that case, raise the Scene Scale in the Paint Effects Globals: Choose F5, Paint Effects > Paint Effects Globals.

3 Paint one or two trees in front of the window on the ground plane. Use the Undo command if you aren't pleased with the positioning or size (see Figure 26.5).

Figure 26.4 In the Trees section, you'll find
▼ *the birch tree animated by wind.*

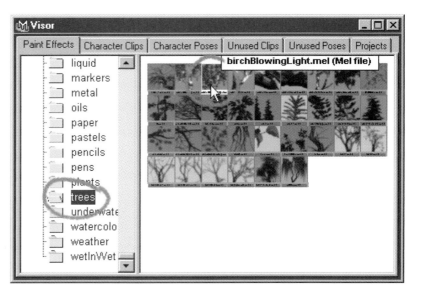

Figure 26.5 A 3D birch tree painted with the Paint Effects brush. ▶

Figure 26.6 Left: the perspective window with the birch tree positioned in front of the window. Right: The rendered view of the tree's shadow in the room. ▼

4 Press the 8 key to leave the Paint Effects. Now you won't see the birch tree(s) any more in a rendered view, only in a schematic display. If necessary, reposition them in the perspective window so they sit close to the window (see Figure 26.6).

5 Render the camera view.

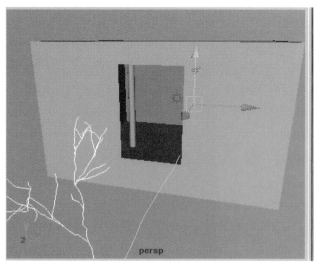

If you've planted your tree well, the sunlight hits the trunk, the branches, and the leaves of the birch and casts nice shadows inside the room. If the shadows only fall outside the building, select the tree and reposition it. Looking through the light is very helpful here.

Remember that 3D animation isn't only about creating cool stuff, it's also about working economically: Why keep the tree in the scene, if all we need are its shadows?

1 Open the tree's Attribute Editor.
2 Click the tab strokeShapebirchBlowingLight1.
3 Uncheck the tree stroke's Primary Visibility (see Figure 26.7).

Primary Visibility means the visibility of an object for rendering. With this parameter switched off, the object is still visible in the modeling views, and its impact on the rest of the scene is also kept. But the object itself won't be rendered (see Figure 26.8). This makes Primary Visibility quite different from the Visibility of an object. If you switch off the Visibility of an object in the Channel Box (or in the Attribute Editor, under Display), the object not only disappears from the modeling and rendered views, but its shadows won't be rendered any more.

The Paint Effects birch tree contains an attribute that gives the tree motion, according to dynamic principles. You don't have to render the sequence to see it, just scrub through the Timeline in the camera view. The Paint Effects force field used here is called Grass Wind. You'll find it (and can edit and key it) by opening the Attribute Editor of the *birchBlowingLight1* node and then the section Tubes in there under Turbulence. Of course, you can create wind for all other kinds of plants, too.

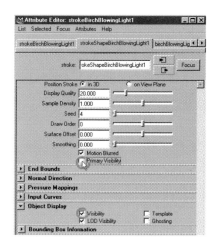

▲ *Figure 26.7 Switching Primary Visibility off will remove the object itself— but not its representation in the modeling views and not its shadows—from the rendering process.*

◄ *Figure 26.8 The shadow of the birch tree in the room. When you render the animation of this view, the leaves and branches move in the wind.*

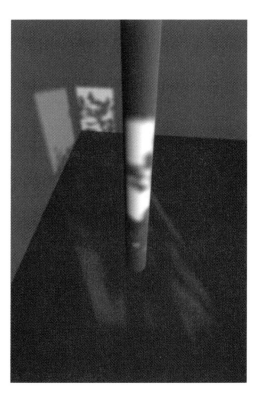

And now for something completely different: Ever thought about the meaning of the icon above the start of the Timeline?

27

How do I animate a glow so that it travels along a ring?
Inspired by Paolo Berto
Theme: Rendering
Techniques and tools used: Hypershader, IPR, Projection

Glow effects are at the top of customers' wishlists when they order 3D animations. Usually they want their most beloved object—toothpaste, a car, stars—to glow so that it attracts extra attention. The 3D animator in this case just opens the Attribute Editor of the toothpaste's material and raises the parameter for *Glow*.

A glow moving along geometry is harder to achieve because you have to get certain parts of the object to glow and not others. Maya renders the glow as a post effect, after it finishes rendering the image. You don't see the glow in the modeling view, so its placement is always a matter of some trial and error. In this tutorial, you'll be able to actually grab the glow in the modeling windows and move it around as you see fit. All we need to accomplish this is a little trick and a brief excursion into the realm of combining texture nodes.

1 Create a ring.

Figure 27.1 A ring—and a change of ▶
layout using a marking menu in the
top of the Hotbox.

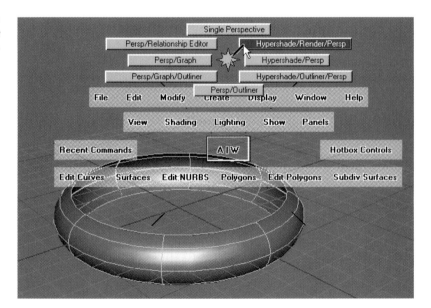

You may use a Nurbs torus and adjust its radii. Or you can create the ring by revolving a Nurbs circle which serves as a cross-section.

2 Assign a Blinn shader to the ring.

A Blinn shader is the typical material to start with when simulating the appearance of metal and its sharp highlights. The most important parameters for the highlight are called *Eccentricity* and *Specular Roll Off*. You'll find them in the Specular Shading section. Instead of tuning a new material you might as well use a fully prepared metal shader from the Internet or from Maya's shader database. Check the Shader Library tab in the Hypershader.

The key to making a glow travel along the ring is to use a local projection of the glow parameter. In other words, we'll project a texture onto the surface that won't change the surface's color but will change the strength of the glow where it hits the surface. It doesn't much matter which kind of texture you use for the glow. We'll use a checker texture because it enables us to estimate the implications of the effect very clearly.

First, it's worth the effort to change the layout of the windows you're working with. Above (some call it "north of") the Hotbox menu set is a marking menu with several preset layouts (see Figure 27.1). The setting Hypershade/Render/Persp is best suited to our purpose. This gives us the perspective window at the bottom right (to put your camera in a good position), and in the window at the bottom left you may continuously run the IPR render process. In the wide top window you have the Hypershader handy for putting your material together (see Figure 27.2).

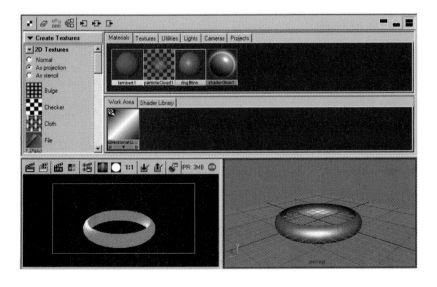

◀ *Figure 27.2 The new layout. At the top is the Hypershader, the toolbox for constructing materials; bottom right is the modeling view; bottom left the continuously updated IPR image.*

3 In the Blinn shader's Attribute Editor, open the section Special Effects and click on the icon next to Glow Intensity. The Create Render Node window opens.

4 In the Create Render Node window, select As projection and the Checker texture (see Figure 27.3).

The IPR window now shows the ring in full glow (see Figure 27.4).

Figure 27.3 Three easy steps from ▶
the material's Attribute Editor and into
the Create Render Node window to let
the checker texture decide where to
put the glow.

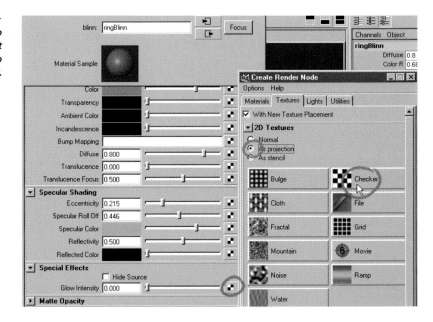

Figure 27.4 The IPR image shows the ▶
glow covering the whole ring. The irregu-
larities stem from the checker texture.

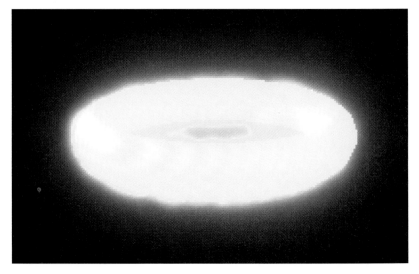

5 In the Hypershader, double-click the checker texture, and in its Attribute Editor darken its value for white: Color1 (Figure 27.5).

This makes the checker pattern clearly visible on the ring. In those parts where the checkerboard shows black, no glow develops. Before we turned the white into gray its massive influence overwhelmed even the nonglowing areas of the ring. Keep in mind that we aren't changing the *color* of the ring, only its glow intensity.

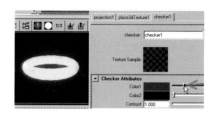

▲ *Figure 27.5 Darkening the white of the checkerboard. The glow renders only in places where the checkerboard shows no black.*

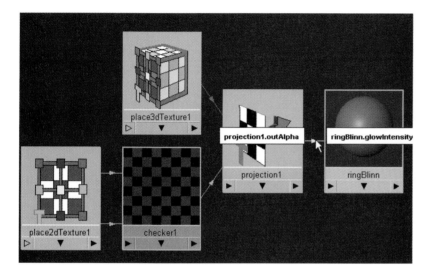

◀ *Figure 27.6 The hierarchical structure of the ring material. The projection through the grayscale distribution (alpha) of* checker1 *determines the intensity of the glow.*

Until now the projection worked on the whole object: It covered all parts of the ring. In order to make the projection work locally we need to dive deep into the logic nodes. Use the Hypershader, click the Work Area tab and right-click or use the icon at the top of the Hypershader window to get Maya to show you the hierarchy of the Blinn material (its up- and downstream connections). When you move your mouse over the connection lines between the nodes, you can see, for example, that *projection1*, the logic node for the projection, sends its grayscale values (its alpha channel information) to the Glow Intensity parameter of the Blinn shader (Figure 27.6).

In the Attribute Editor of *projection1*, change the following three settings:

1 Change the projection type from Normal to Cylinder.
2 Under the section Color Balance, set the Default Color to black.
3 Under the section Effects, switch off the parameter Wrap (see Figure 27.7).

Wrap causes the texture to wrap around the whole object (or repeat continuously over the whole object). When it's deactivated the checker (or any kind of texture) works exactly where we want it to—and nowhere else. At parts of the object where the material doesn't find any texture information,

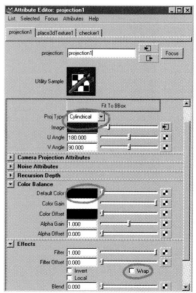

▲ *Figure 27.7 Three changes in the Attribute Editor of the projection restrict the glow to local.*

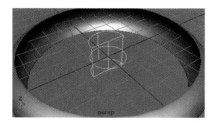

Figure 27.8 With the Wrap parameter ▲ turned off, the ring only glows in places where it's being hit by the green place3dTexture object.

it will bring the Default Color forward. We want our material to be black wherever there's no glow and light gray or even white where there should be a glow.

If you check the perspective window, you'll see a green, half-closed wireframe cylinder at the center of the scene (see Figure 27.8). This object is called *place3dTexture1* and won't be rendered. All it does is describe where the glow should appear and where not. Since it currently sits in the middle of the ring, the IPR window shows us no glow at all.

1 Translate, rotate, and scale the texture-placement icon *place3dTexture1* so that it covers a small part of the ring (see Figure 27.9).

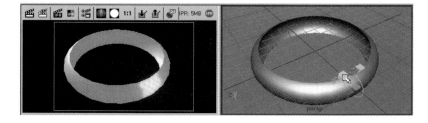

Figure 27.9 The IPR window shows ▶ the glowing checker texture at work very locally. To the right: the manipulator handles of the placement node.

The render window shows you the desired glow effect only at the designated part of the ring. In order to apply the local glow more accurately, try the other manipulator handles of the texture icon.

2 Move the pivot (Insert key) of *place3dTexture1* to the center of the scene (see Figure 27.10). Use the X key for grid snapping.

3 Animate the rotation parameter of *place3dTexture1* with keyframes or an expression, so that the glow winds around the whole ring several times (see Figure 27.11).

Figure 27.10 Moving the texture ▶ placement node's pivot to the center of the ring.

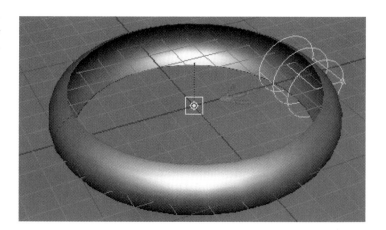

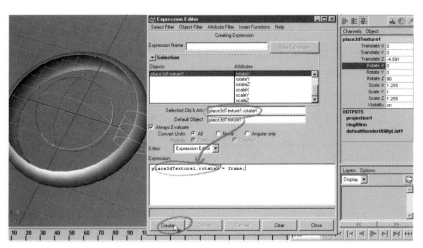

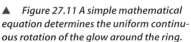

▲   *Figure 27.11 A simple mathematical equation determines the uniform continuous rotation of the glow around the ring.*

Figure 27.12 Back to the ▶ familiar Four View layout.

If you're not pleased with the checker texture and the glow seems too weak for your taste, set both colors of the checker texture to a similar—and maybe brighter—value of gray. If you want to change the color (or other properties) of the glow itself, open the Hypershader and double-click the node *ShaderGlow1*. This node—not the checker texture—determines the main look of the glow. If you want to return to the normal Four View, use the new icons of Maya 4 at the lower-left border of the screen.

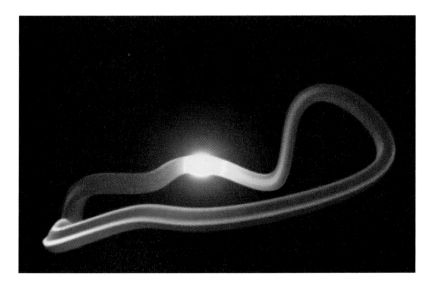

◀   *Figure 27.13 Animation of the glow along a more complex surface. Here the texture placement icon was attached to a path along the surface and so follows the shape precisely.*

And now for something completely different: Ever used the middle mouse button to scrub through the Timeline in an animation?

28

SWIM RING WITH LOVE

How do I paint six hearts at distinct places on an inflatable swim ring?
Theme: Rendering
Techniques and tools used: 3D Paint Tool, Paint Effects

Previously, software that enabled us to paint directly on 3D objects was expensive. With version 3 of Maya it became more affordable, and with Maya 4 it isn't a problem any more: 3D painting is now fully integrated into the software. With the 3D Paint Tool you can even use Paint Effects brushes to paint directly on Nurbs or polygon surfaces.

However, painting directly on 3D geometry has always had restrictions, especially when painting details. It's easier—and certainly more precise—to paint in 2D. That's why we'll use a procedure here that combines the strengths of painting in 3D with the strengths of painting in 2D.

What we'll do is paint a rough outline of the 3D texture directly onto an object and later refine it in the 2D mode of the Paint Effects. We'll see the result immediately in the IPR image. Our object of choice will be a torus—let's call it a swim ring—which we'll decorate with six red hearts.

1 Create a Nurbs torus. Raise its radius to 5 and reduce its height ratio to 0.3.
2 Assign a new material to the torus.
3 Select the torus.
4 Switch to rendering (F5) and call up the tool for painting in 3D: Choose Textures > 3D Paint Tool. This tool can only be used reasonably with its option window.
5 Assign a file texture to the swim ring by clicking Assign Textures in the 3D Paint Tool window, under File Textures. In the new window that opens, give the texture a reasonable size of 512 x 512 pixels (see Figure 28.1).

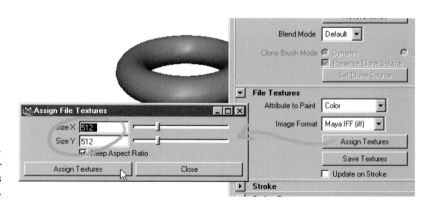

Figure 28.1 A torus, ready to be ▶ painted on. The 3D Paint window asks for the size of the texture and 512 x 512 is the minimum for our needs.

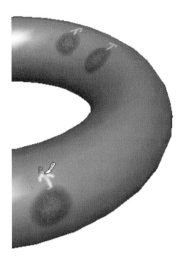

Figure 28.2 Painting in 3D. ▶
The swim ring receives six red dots where the hearts will be painted later.

◀ *Figure 28.3 Arrows painted with a smaller brush mark which way is up.*

6 In the 3D Paint Tool window, set Radius (U) to a smaller size, select a color, and paint six dots at six places of the swim ring (see Figure 28.2).

7 With an even finer brush and another color, paint arrows pointing upward from the dots (see Figure 28.3). This will make it easy for you later in the 2D image to figure out where the tops of the hearts are supposed to be.

8 Save the scene.

It's important to save here because in the next step Maya will save the texture you painted, which is currently still in the computer's RAM, into your project's directory on your hard drive. Maya will use the scene name to generate the image name.

9 In the 3D Paint Tool window, click Save Textures. Make a note of the entry in the Command Feedback line at the bottom right of the Maya window.

Here you see the name under which the file texture is being saved. In your current project, you'll find a folder called *3dPaintTextures*. This folder contains a folder with the name of your scene, and in it is an image named *nurbsTorusShape1_color.iff*. If you open it with fcheck you'll see an image that is somewhat similar in color to the picture you previously painted directly onto the ring in 3D, but the dots and arrows seem to have strange positions and relationships to each other (see Figure 28.4). If you had painted a circle around the top and the bottom of the ring you would

Figure 28.4 What does this 2D picture have to do with the 3D texture ▼ *we painted? A lot!*

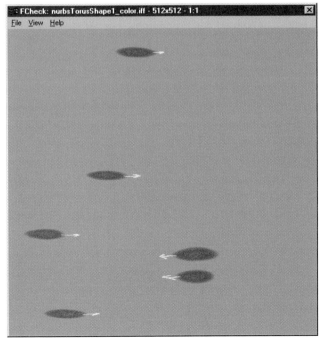

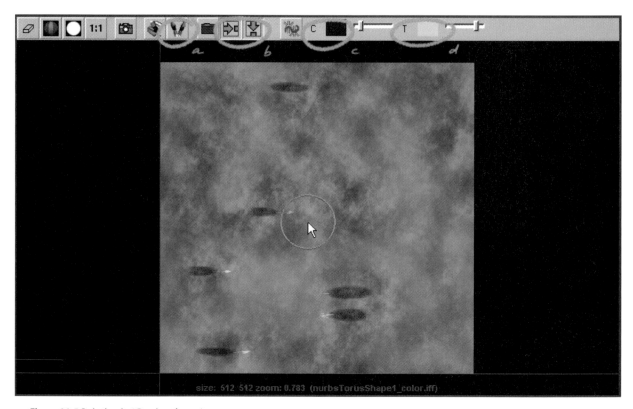

*Figure 28.5 Painting in 2D using the ▲
Paint Effects. The most important buttons
in the header of the window: a) gets a
new brush, b) toggles texture wrapping
between horizontal and vertical,
c) changes color, and d)
changes the transparency.*

now see these two circles in 2D as straight vertical lines. These things, which can puzzle beginners, are very familiar to texturing experts and can bring the 2D and 3D worlds together easily.

When dealing with polygon objects, we can rearrange textures in 2D at a very local level, according to the distribution of polygon faces. With Nurbs surfaces, we have to stick to the global structure of their U/V mapping and can't change details at a local level of geometry. What we can do, however—and will do at this point—is load this 2D image into the Paint Effects and clean it up there. This allows for very detailed work.

1 Use the key 8 to switch to the Paint Effects.
2 Switch from Paint > Paint Scene (painting in 3D) to Paint > Paint Canvas (painting in 2D).
3 Choose Canvas > Open Image to open your texture file (see Figure 28.5).
4 Repaint the image with the Paint Effects. Where the dots are, paint hearts. Use the arrows for orientation (see Figures 28.6 through 28.9).

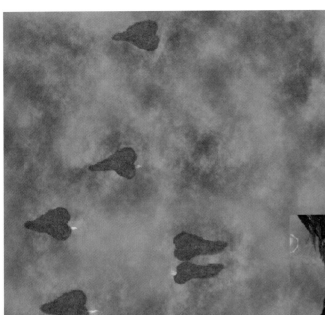

◀   *Figure 28.6 First try. The hearts were painted with digital red oil, the blue comes from the Paint Effects' Clouds.*

Figure 28.7 Add a couple of 3D sunflowers on
▼   *the flat canvas.*

◀   *Figure 28.8 In the rendered image the hearts look too wide and the sunflowers are stretched.*

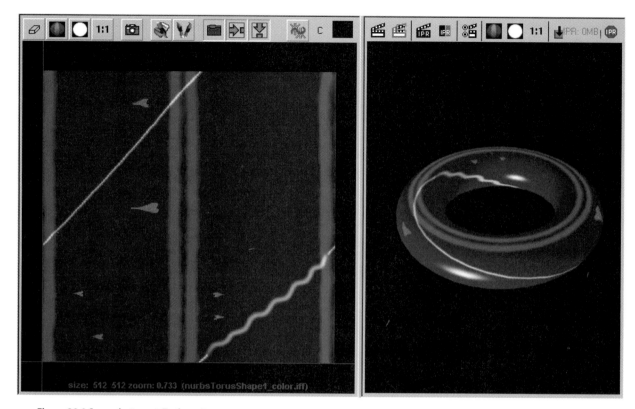

_Figure 28.9 Second attempt. To the ▲
left is the 2D image with the hearts
purposely stretched longer and clearer
line structures. These structures remain
clear in the rendered image (right), where
the hearts appear in normal proportions._

_Figure 28.10 The color texture is ▶
being used as a bump map as well.
Where lighter color tones are present,
the geometry seems to stick out slightly._

Hints for Using Maya's Paint Effects to Paint in 2D

● I recommend a window setup where on the right you see the continuously updated IPR image of the perspective camera and on the left you have the actual Paint Effects window for your work in 2D.

● When painting on canvas (in 2D) the Undo command (key Z) doesn't work. There is only one undo step, which you can invoke from the Canvas menu. The Paint Effects are a pretty stable program module, but saving (under different names) is nevertheless a good habit. The Save command for 2D images is also in the Canvas menu.

● Also in the Canvas menu you'll find the command Auto Save. If you activate it, Maya will save every stroke so that you can immediately see its effect in the perspective (and IPR) window.

● While working on canvas, use the navigation options with the ALT key, for example to get a closer look at your image and see more detail.

● A very helpful tool (standard in 2D applications) is the pipette. It isn't directly available in the Paint Effects window, but you can access it with the Color Chooser, which always opens whenever you click on the color field next to the letter C in the header of the Paint Effects window.

● Next to the C is the T, which determines the transparency of the current paint brush. Select a light gray to apply a color lightly and black if you want to work with an opaque brush that covers everything underneath.

● A very helpful shortcut for resizing the brush is the B key. Hold this key down, press the left mouse button, and move the mouse right to make the stroke larger or left to make it smaller.

● Make use of the large selection of brushes, especially the 2D brushes such as those in the Oil and Watercolor sections. Although 3D brushes can also be attractive, keep in mind that they bring with them their own very strong lighting behavior. When you apply them to a 3D object, you get false lighting conditions because the internal brush lighting mixes with the actual 3D lights in your scene.

● Wrap Canvas is a very useful effect, which you can reach through the two arrow icons in the header of the Paint Effects window. It simulates a continuously repeating wallpaper, so when you move your brush off the canvas on one side, it reappears on the other side. This is important with textures applied to topologically endless surfaces like a sphere or torus.

● Note that when painting in 2D you can derive variants of your color images as maps for the specular color or for a bump map (see Figure 28.10).

And now for something completely different: When in translation mode ever Ctrl-clicked on the blue translation arrow?

RENDERING

How do I make a series of letters move in front of a lens with a changing refractive index?
Theme: Rendering
Techniques and tools used: Text, Raytracing, Refractive Index

Flying logos are certainly passé, but pleasantly animated 2D typography has a timeless beauty. Very nice effects can be achieved by animating objects (and not just letters) as they move in front of a lens. Even more interesting structures will evolve if the lens changes its refractive index and acts, so to speak, rubbery.

In order to render refracting light, we have to drop the usual render procedure Maya provides for us and switch to *Raytracing*. Raytracing shoots countless digital rays into the 3D scene, calculates how these rays are being reflected or refracted by the surfaces they reach, and at the end of this lengthy calculation delivers an image that looks hyperrealistically sharp and detailed.

1 Choose Create > Text and use the option window to create text in the type font and size of your choice (see Figure 29.1). Since you want to render the letters, don't just create curves, but activate Trim (for Nurbs surfaces) or Poly (for polygon surfaces).

The letters appear as a group of objects in the scene. You may delete the curves from which the text was created and give the letters color.

Figure 29.1 Text creation: Here we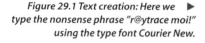
type the nonsense phrase "r@ytrace moi!"
using the type font Courier New.

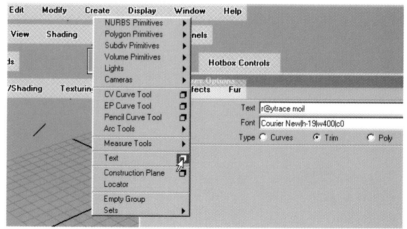

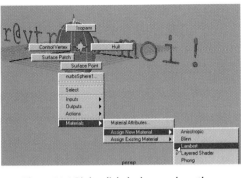

▲ *Figure 29.2 Right-click the lens and use the context menu to give it a new Lambert material. The text received a procedural texture.*

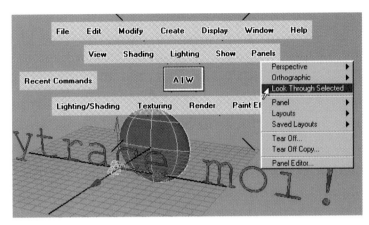

▲ *Figure 29.3 The lens sits in front of the camera. When looking through the camera in the modeling view we see a wall of gray.*

2 Put a sphere into the scene and scale it flat so that it resembles the shape of a lens.

3 Assign a Lambert shader to the lens (see Figure 29.2).

4 Create a new camera by choosing Create > Cameras > Camera or by clicking on the camera icon in the shelf.

5 Select the lens, followed by the camera, and press the P key.

The P key parents the lens to the camera ("Very convenient," jokes my friend, a cinematographer who mounts lens systems on camera bodies every day).

6 Move the lens slightly forward, away from the camera. Look through the camera (see Figure 29.3).

The camera looks at a gray lens and therefore doesn't see the letters any more.

7 Open the Attribute Editor of the lens's Lambert shader and drag the slider for Transparency all the way to the right.

This makes the lens (visible in the modeling view as well as in rendering) completely transparent.

There are two steps to using raytracing. First, you have to tell the material that it will participate in the raytracing process. By doing this, you can decide which specific objects (or more precisely, which materials) will participate in the time-consuming rendering process and which will not. Second, you have to activate the Raytracing option in the general render settings, the Render Globals.

1 Open the Lambert shader's Attribute Editor, and in the Raytrace Options section, activate Refractions (see Figure 29.4).

2 Open the Render Globals. In the Raytracing Quality section, switch on Raytracing.

Figure 29.4 Left: The Hypershader. ▶
Right: The attributes of the lens material.
The transparency is set to full and the
ability to refract light is switched on.

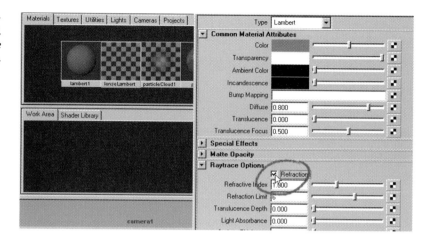

When you render the view through the camera (IPR unfortunately doesn't work with raytracing), the letters of the phrase just appear normal and undistorted (see Figure 29.5). This is because the refractive index of the lens is *1*, meaning that all rays that run from the letters, through the lens, and into the camera are left unchanged.

Figure 29.5 Raytracing without ray ▲
deflection. The refractive index of the lens
is at its default value of 1.

3 In the Lambert shader's Attribute Editor, change the Refractive Index from its default value of *1* to a higher value, such as *1.3*.

4 Render the scene again.

Now you can see the effect of refracted light (Figure 29.6).

5 Change the camera position and vary the refractive index of the lens (see Figure 29.7). Also play with the distance between the lens and the camera.

Figure 29.6 The text, rendered with ▶
a refractive index of 1.3.

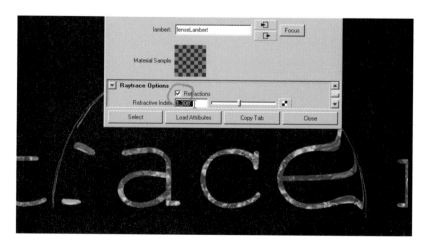

▲ *Figure 29.7 Bizarre 2D shapes, achieved by stronger refractions. Only the letters to the right of the lens appear normal.*

Before you move the lens, which sits in the coordinate system of the camera, double-click the icon of the translation tool or call up its option window. In the Tool Setting window, select the Object mode. Usually you move objects around a scene in World mode, which uses a coordinate system parallel to the XYZ axes of the scene.

From here on, you have many choices for animating the logomotion. You can move the letters past the camera or you can animate the camera to run past the letters. Most importantly, you should animate the refractive index (see Figure 29.8). You can use the Channel Box for this: Right-click the words Refractive Index and set the key. Values above 1 make the lens become a magnifying glass. At much higher values, the image flips.

◀ *Figure 29.8 Animation of the refractive lens. Refractive Index settings, from top to bottom: 0.3, 0.8, 1.0, 1.2, 1.5, 2.0, 2.3.*

And now for something completely different: Ever used Optimize Scene to clean up all the mess?

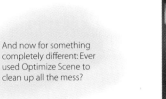

How do I animate a calligraphic brush painting ji, the Chinese character for machine?
With thanks to Li-yun Bauer-Hsieh and to Huang Song
Theme: Rendering
Techniques and tools used: Paint Effects, Clip, Trax Editor

Figure 30.1 "Space shuttle" ▲
in Chinese: " a space-penetrating shuttle machine." The sign at the far right represents the abbreviated, modern way of writing ji (machine).

A basic difference between all previous digital painting methods and Maya's Paint Effects is that in common paint packages the stroke is frozen once painted, whereas every completed Paint Effects stroke can later be adjusted, changed, and—yes!—animated. You just might want to take a look at all the (keyable) attributes of a simple ink stroke in Maya—it's astounding.

Figure 30.2 Painting the character ji ▶
traditionally with a calligraphic brush.

In this tutorial, we'll animate a single Chinese ideogram, *ji* (machine). The Chinese word for space shuttle, for example, contains the character ji. Space shuttle is *taikong chuan suoji* —a shuttle machine penetrating space. Ji, the last character in this term, is written shorthand these days, in the modern system of writing. However, the original character, thousands of years old, is much more complex (see Figure 30.3). It basically consists of four parts: to the left (strokes 1 through 4), wood; at the top right (strokes 5 through 10), two shuttles of a loom or a door locker representing moving mechanical parts; below in the middle (strokes 11 through 13), man; and finally the large structure cutting through the whole right part of the sign (strokes 14 through 16), the weapon. Reading this as a sentence, we get "moving wooden mechanical parts that help man fight."

In the art of calligraphy, the order and direction in which every stroke is placed on paper is very important. Since it's a dynamic process, describing it on static paper using numbers and arrows like in Figure 30.3 is not exactly adequate. With an animation, however, this information can be conveyed in a very concise and intuitive way. We'll use a calligraphic brush and animate the strokes after we painted them. (If you have a graphic tablet, use it!) It will be easy to coordinate the animation of all the different strokes using non-linear animation and the Trax Editor.

1 Create a Nurbs surface.

2 Make it 3 units large.

Figure 30.4 Clicking the Get Brush ▲
icon in the Paint Effects window opens the
Visor. The calligraphic brush is located in
the folder of pens.

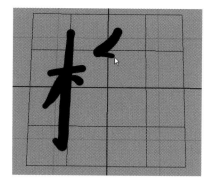

Figure 30.5 Calligraphic painting ▲
using the Paint Effects.

Figure 30.6 On the left are the ▶
16 painted strokes in the meager
representation of the perspective
window. In the middle is the Outliner with
the whole list of strokes. On the right is
the Channel Box. The two crucial attributes
for animating strokes are marked:
Max Clip and Primary Visibility.

3 With F5, switch to Rendering.
4 Make the (still selected) surface ready to paint: Choose Paint Effects > Make Paintable.

All of this creates a surface and prepares it for the calligraphic brush, which we'll choose now.

1 Press the 8 key. This brings you to the Paint Effects.
2 Click on the icon for Get Brush. The Visor opens.
3 In the Visor, open the folder with the pens.
4 Click on the brush called *calligraphic.mel* (see Figure 30.4).
5 Close the Visor.
6 On the paper, draw the 16 strokes forming the character ji, according to the hand-painted illustration in Figure 30.3. Follow the numbers and arrows as closely as possible. Take your time (see Figure 30.5).
7 Leave the Paint Effects by pressing the 8 key again.

The perspective window shows the calligraphic strokes as curves on the surface (see Figure 30.6). In the Outliner, we see the individual curves as a list of objects. In the Channel Box, under the strokeShape Calligraphic section we find the attribute Max Clip. This attribute is crucial for our animation. If we reduce its value, we shorten the stroke. At the very bottom of the section we find the attribute Primary Visibility, which allows us to exclude a stroke from being rendered.

We will now keyframe all strokes so they're invisible at the beginning of the animation by setting their Primary Visibility to off. One frame later, they'll all become visible (Primary Visibility on) and stand at the beginning of their paths (Max Clip 0). At the end of the animation, they'll reach the ends of their paths and appear fully developed (Max Clip 1).

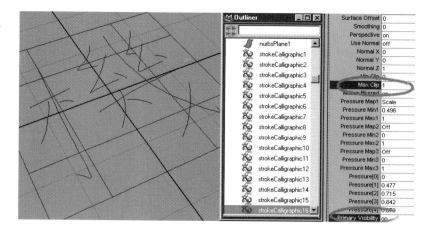

1 Prepare an animation length of 200 frames.
2 Go to the beginning of the animation.
3 In the Outliner, select all strokes.

The Channel Box lists the attributes of all selected strokes but shows only the attributes of the last selected stroke (see Figure 30.7). So, don't worry about this.

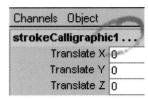

▲ *Figure 30.7 The Channel Box indicates (by three dots after the name of the stroke) that this isn't the only object currently selected.*

4 In the Channel Box, type the word *off* next to the field Primary Visibility. Right-click the words Primary Visibility and key the selected parameter.
5 Step one frame forward.
6 Switch on Primary Visibility (by typing *on*) and set a keyframe.
7 Reduce the value of Max Clip from 1 to 0 and set a keyframe.
8 Go to the end of the animation.
9 Enter the value 1 for Max Clip and set the last keyframe.

Now all 16 strokes have three keyframes each. If you render the animation at the start frame you get an empty sheet of paper (see Figure 30.8). Rendering the next frame, you see all strokes at their beginning state (see Figure 30.9). If you run the animation, you see the strokes develop uniformly and simultaneously reach their full length at the end (see Figure 30.10). If you painted a stroke the wrong direction, you could fix it now by animating Max Clip from 1 to 0 instead of from 0 to 1, while retaining 1 as the value of Min Clip.

▲ *Figure 30.8 The rendered animation at frame 0.*

▲ *Figure 30.9 The rendered animation at frame 100: All strokes develop simultaneously.*

▲ *Figure 30.10 At frame 200 all strokes reach their full lengths at the same time.*

Now it's timing time! (Who said traxin' time?) Nothing works better for changing the timing than the tools of nonlinear animation. This is a straightforward procedure. We'll first convert all animations to clips and then scale them and shove them around in the Trax Editor to achieve the appropriate timing. If your current version of Maya doesn't support nonlinear animation, use the Dope Sheet for these final touches.

The strokes we see listed in the Outliner don't actually contain the keyframes we just set. If we tried to convert them into clips the software would return an error message due to nonexistent animation data. What we see in the Outliner is the information about the curves. The information about the shapes of the strokes is called *strokeShapes* and lives in logic nodes below the curves. So what we'll convert into clips now is not the strokes but the strokeShapes.

1 In the Outliner or in the perspective window, select the first stroke. Press the down arrow key to go one step down in the hierarchy, to the shapes.
2 Switch to Animation (F2).
3 Choose Animate > Create Clip. This converts the keyframes of the selected object into a clip.
4 Select the second stroke, press the down arrow key again, followed by the G key (repeat last command). The Command Feedback line tells you that Maya has just created *clip2*.
5 Proceed in the same way with all the remaining strokes. Within a minute or so you should have generated 16 clips.

Playing back the animation you won't notice much change: All the strokes—long or short—develop simultaneously during 200 frames. One change is noticeable, however: The timeline doesn't show keyframes any more. Now we find the keyframes packed together in compact bars, one below the other in the Trax Editor, where we can easily manipulate them for our needs.

6 Choose Window > Animation Editors to open the Trax Editor (see Figure 30.11).
7 Select all clips. Then double-click one of them.

This brings all parameters of all selected clips into the Channel Box. We'll now reduce the length of the bars.

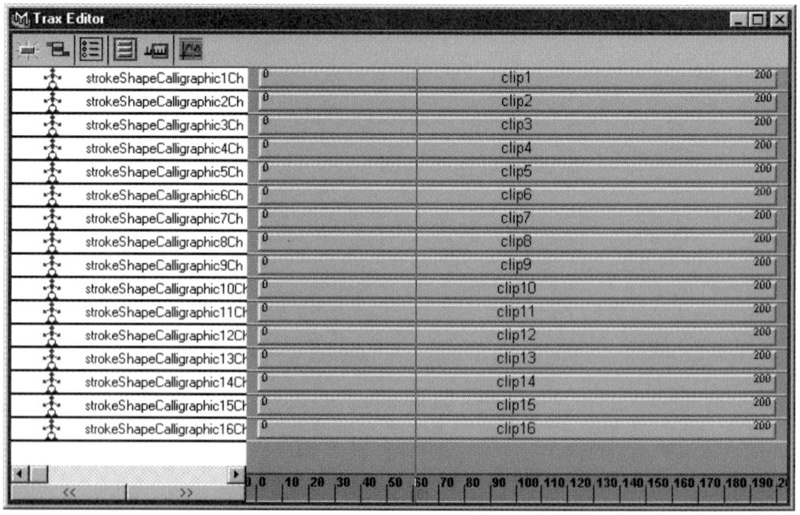

Figure 30.11 A clear view of the Trax ▶
Editor, where all animation data are
shown as bars, all starting at frame 0
and all ending at frame 200.

8 In the Channel Box, reduce the Scale of all strokes, by entering the value 0.2.

This makes the clips one-fifth their original length, in this case, less than two seconds instead of eight seconds (counted in PAL or film).

9 Move the clips in the Trax Editor so that one follows another in time (see Figure 30.12). Use the standard navigation possibilities provided by the ALT key.

When you run the animation (you may have to widen the playback range), you'll see the result of these few nonlinear manipulations. The first stroke develops. When it's finished, the second one starts, and so on.

If you were creating this animation for a teaching medium like an interactive CD-ROM you would have to do some extra editing now. For example, it would be wise to slightly separate the four parts of the character ji from each other in time and give the shorter strokes less time than the longer ones to develop to their full lengths. If you want, you can also animate the surface where all this happens, and apply a paper texture to it. This texture is independent from the calligraphic strokes. You can even change (and animate) the look of individual strokes by opening their Attribute Editor. For example, try a Gap Size value of 0.7 (see Figure 30.13).

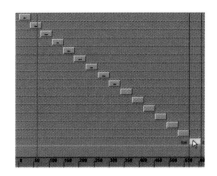

▲ *Figure 30.12 Shortening and moving clips just like in digital video editing.*

◀ *Figure 30.13 Stroke 14 with color and gap values changed.*

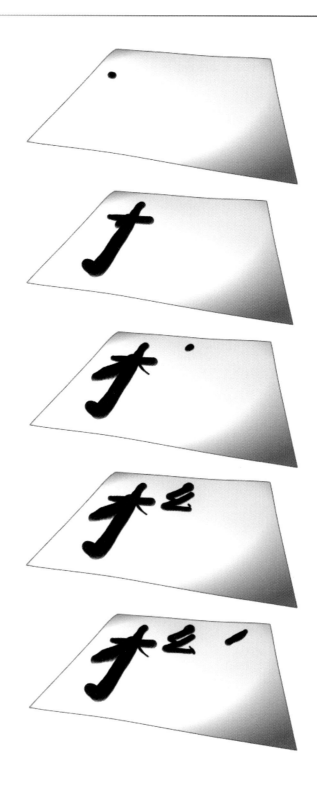

And now for something completely different: Ever clicked the right mouse button in the Timeline?

INDEX